CONGREGATION FOR INSTITUTES
OF CONSECRATED LIFE
AND SOCIETIES OF APOSTOLIC LIFE

CONTEMPLATE
Year of Consecrated Life

"You whom my heart loves" (*Song* 1:7)

To consecrated men and women
on the path of Beauty

*All documents are published thanks to the generous support
of the members of the Catholic Truth Society*

CATHOLIC TRUTH SOCIETY
PUBLISHERS TO THE HOLY SEE

CONTEMPLATE
YEAR OF CONSECRATED LIFE

"You whom my heart loves" (*Song* 1:7)

To consecrated men and women on the path of Beauty

"Authentic love is always contemplative"
(Pope Francis)

CONTENTS

Dearest brothers and sisters 7

PROLOGUE. 9
    Listening 11
    Consecrated life, *statio orante* in the heart of history 13

SEEKING. 21
    Listening 23
    The everyday apprenticeship of seeking. 24
        Pilgrims to the core 26
        Quaerere Deum 27
    The search in the night 28
        Desire 29
        Hope 30

DWELLING. 33
    Listening 35
    In the form of Beauty 37
        The Beauty that wounds 40
        The Beauty that renews 44
    An exercise of truth. 46
        Holiness that welcomes 46
        The listening that sees 47
        Quies, requies, otium 49
        The ineffable memory. 51

FORMATION ... 55

Listening ... 57
Beauty's way of living ... 58
  Mystical pedagogy ... 59
  Paschal pedagogy ... 61
  The pedagogy of beauty ... 62
  The pedagogy of thought ... 65
Mercy is close by ... 68
In the dance of creation ... 71
  A new philokalia ... 72

EPILOGUE ... 75

Listening ... 77
On the mountain, in the sign of fulfilment ... 78
On the way to God's safekeeping ... 82

FOR REFLECTION ... 87

Hail, Woman clothed with the sun ... 91

First published 2016 by The Incorporated Catholic Truth Society 40-46 Harleyford Road London SE11 5AY Tel: 020 7640 0042 Fax: 020 7640 0046. Copyright © 2015 Libreria Editrice Vaticana, Citta del Vaticano.

ISBN 978 1 78469 075 5

Dearest brothers and sisters,

1. The Year of Consecrated Life - a precious and blessed journey - has crossed its zenith, while the voices of consecrated men and women from every part of the world express the joy of vocation and fidelity to their identity in the Church, a testimony that sometimes leads to martyrdom.

The two letters *Rejoice* and *Keep Watch* launched a journey of shared reflection, serious and significant, that raised existential questions for our life as individuals and as members of an institute. It is proper now to continue our common reflection, and fix our gaze on the heart of our life of *discipleship*.

Let us direct our gaze into the depths of our life, seeking the reasons underlying our pilgrimage in search of God, and examine the contemplative dimension of our lives so we may recognise the mystery of grace that sustains us, exhilarates us and transfigures us.

Pope Francis calls us with eager concern to turn the gaze of our life to Jesus, but also allow him to look at us in order "to realise ever anew that we have been entrusted with a treasure which makes us more human and helps us to lead a new life".[1] He invites us to train the gaze of our heart because "true love is always contemplative".[2] The theological relationship of the consecrated person with the Lord (*confessio Trinitatis*), fraternal communion with those who are called to live the same charism (*signum fraternitatis*), and mission as revelation of God's merciful love amidst the human community (*servitium caritatis*): all this comes back to the never-exhausted search for the face of God, to obedient listening to his Word, in order to reach the contemplation of the living and true God.

The various forms of consecrated life - eremitic and virginal, monastic and canonical, conventual and apostolic, secular and new fraternities - drink from the spring of contemplation, refresh themselves at it and receive strength. In it they encounter the mystery that dwells within them and find fulness for living the evangelical paradigm of consecration, communion, and mission.

---

[1] Pope Francis, apostolic exhortation *Evangelii Gaudium* (24th November 2013), 264.
[2] Ibid., 199.

This letter - which carries on from the instruction *The Contemplative Dimension of Religious Life* (1980), the post-synodal apostolic exhortation *Vita Consecrata* (1996), the apostolic letter *Novo millennio ineunte* (2001), and the instructions *Starting Afresh from Christ* (2002) and *Faciem tuam, Domine, requiram* (2008) - comes to you, therefore, as an invitation opening onto the mystery of God, the foundation of our whole life. This is an invitation that opens before us a horizon never to be reached and never fully mastered: our relationship with the secret of the living God, the primacy of life in the Spirit, the communion of love with Jesus, the centre of life and constant source of every initiative,[3] a living experience that demands to be shared.[4] The desire resounds: *Set me as a seal upon your heart* (*Song* 8:6).

The Holy Spirit who alone knows and moves within our depths, *intimior intimo meo*,[5] accompanies us in this truth-telling, building-up and transforming of our lives, so that it may welcome and rejoice in a Presence that dwells within is, desired and loved, a true *confessio Trinitatis* in the Church and in the human city: "We make ourselves all the more ready to receive it when we have more faith in believing it, more firmness in hoping in it, more ardour in desiring it".[6]

The mystical cry that recognises the Beloved, *You are the fairest of the sons of men* (*Ps* 45:3), as the power of love makes the Church fruitful and, in the human city, reassembles Beauty's lost and broken fragments.

---

[3] Cf. Congregation for Institutes of Consecrated Life and Societies of Apostolic Life, instruction *Starting Afresh from Christ: A Renewed Commitment to Consecrated Life in the Third Millennium* (19th May 2002), 22.

[4] Cf. John Paul II, post-synodal apostolic exhortation *Vita Consecrata* (25th March 1996), 16.

[5] Cf. St Augustine, *Confessions* III, 6, 11.

[6] Ibid., *Ep* 130, 8, 17.

PROLOGUE

*Through the streets and through the squares;
I want to seek the beloved of my heart.*

(Song of Songs, 3:2)

LISTENING

2. A person who loves is imbued with a power, experiences the Paschal nature of existence, and accepts the risk of leaving self in order to encounter the other - not only in an external place, but also on the inside; and discovers that his own good consists in dwelling within the other and welcoming him into oneself. Love directs a new gaze toward others, a gaze of special intimacy, by virtue of which the other person does not remain on the level of ideas, does not stay at the threshold, but enters into the private world of our own feelings to the point of becoming *the beloved of my heart* (*Song* 3:2), "the one I have sought".

This is the dynamism that permeates the *Song of Songs* (in Hebrew, *šîr haššîrîm*), a book so superlative as to be called the "holy of holies" of the First Testament. It is the first of the five scrolls (*meghillôt*) that have a special liturgical significance for Jews: it is read during the celebration of Passover itself. This sublime song celebrates the beauty and attractive power of the love between man and woman, which blossoms within a story composed of desire, seeking, encounter, and which becomes *exodus* by going out through the *streets* and *squares* (*Song* 3:2) and kindles in the world the fire of the love of God. If human love is presented in the book as a *divine flame* (*Song* 8:6; *alhebetyâ*), the flame of *Yāh*, it is because it is *the most sublime way* (*1 Cor* 12:31) It is the reality without which man is *nothing* (*1 Cor* 13:2), it is the thing that brings the creature closest to God. Love is the resonance and fruit of God's very nature. The creature who loves is humanised, but at the same time also experiences the beginning of a process of divinisation because *God is love* (*1 John* 4:10,16). The creature who loves is striving toward fulness and peace, toward *šalom*, which is the harbour of communion, just as it is for the spouses of the *Song* who bear this *šalom* in their name, he is *Šelōmōh*, she *Šûlammît* (the Shulamite).

The *Song* has been interpreted in a literal way, as a celebration of the power of the human love between a woman and a man, but also in an allegorical way, in the great Jewish and Christian tradition, as speaking of the relationship between God and Israel, Christ and the Church. The book, however, finds its fulcrum in the spousal dynamic of love. In the manner of a parable which helps to move us into a different place where we speak the living language of lovers that heals the wounds of solitude, dejection, and selfishness, it leads us back into the present moment by suggesting to us that life does not progress by the imposing of commands or constraints, nor by means of rules; but by virtue of an ecstasy, an enchantment, a rapture that takes us out of ourselves, sets us on a journey and reads history from a perspective of relationship, communion, and *agape*.

This spousal love, that engages all the senses and inspires the steps of the journey: the human creature can live it not only toward another human being, but also toward God. This is what happens to a person who is consecrated to God in the wisdom-bearing setting and the fertile atmosphere of the evangelical counsels, focussed on proclaiming the primacy of a relationship with him. This is why the *Song* is a shining beacon for the consecrated.

The *Song*, defined as a hymn of unitive mysticism, can also be read as the journey of the heart on its way to God, as an existential pilgrimage toward the encounter with the God made flesh who loves nuptially. It can be read as a symphony of spousal love, encompassing the disquiet of the search for the beloved (*dôd*), the arrival at the encounter that satisfies the heart, and the savouring of choice and mutual belonging.

In the light of the *Song*, consecrated life appears as a vocation to the love that thirsts for the living God (*Ps* 42:3; 63:2), that kindles in the world the search for the hidden God (*1 Ch* 16:11; *Ps* 105:4; *Is* 55:6; *Am* 5:6; *Zeph* 2:3), and that encounters him in the faces of the brethren (*Mt* 25:40). It is there that God finds room to pitch his tent (*Rev* 21:3): in prayer or in the depths of the heart where God loves to live (*Gal* 2:20). Consecrated men and women move towards Christ in order to encounter his words that are *spirit and life* (*Jn* 6:63). They are intent on finding him in sacred places, but also *in the streets and in the squares* (*Song* 3:2), and are deputised to make the personal encounter with his love a passion that intercedes in history.

Prologue

CONSECRATED LIFE, *STATIO ORANTE* IN THE HEART OF HISTORY

3. Pope Francis writes, in the apostolic letter addressed to consecrated men and women: "I expect that each form of consecrated life will question what it is that God and people today are asking of them. . . . Only by such concern for the needs of the world, and by docility to the promptings of the Spirit, will this Year of Consecrated Life become an authentic *kairos*, a time rich in God's grace, a time of transformation".[7]

It is a question that echoes within each of us. The pope offers an initial response: "We are called to know and show that God is able to fill our hearts to the brim with happiness; that we need not seek our happiness elsewhere."[8]

Desiring fulness and seeking happiness, impassioned but never satiated with joy, we all share this restlessness.

We are seeking the true joy (cf. *Jn* 15:11) at "a time in which forgetfulness of God is becoming habitual, a time in which the fundamental act of the human personality tends to pronounce itself for its own absolute autonomy, exempting itself from every transcendent law; a time, moreover, in which expressions of the spirit reach summits of irrationality and desolation; a time, finally, that sees even in the great ethnic religions of the world disturbances and decadence not experienced before".[9]

These are words that Blessed Paul VI addressed to the world in the course of the last public session of the Second Vatican Council. Our time, even more than the years immediately after the Council, is characterised by the paradigmatic centrality of change and has as its characteristic elements speed, relativity, and complexity. Everything changes at a faster pace than in the past, and this causes disorientation and disquiet in those who remain anchored to ancient certainties and to old ways of interpreting reality. This acceleration makes the present volatile: the present is a place of emotions, of encounters, of temporary choices, while what is needed is stability and solid ground for judgement and for living.

---

[7] Pope Francis, apostolic letter *To All Consecrated People*, on the occasion of the Year of Consecrated Life (21st November 2014), II, 5.

[8] Ibid., II, 1.

[9] Paul VI, allocution on the occasion of the last public session of the Second Vatican Council, 7th December 1965.

The superabundance of events, communication, and experiences, makes summarising and discernment difficult, which is why many cannot live a search for meaning so as to make the present a place to discover understanding, communion, and sharing.

The present culture, especially in the West, is focussed mainly on practice, entirely bent on doing and producing, and generates as a consequence an unexamined need for silence, listening, and a contemplative breathing-space. These two contrasting conditions, however, threaten to establish a greater superficiality. Both activism and certain ways of living contemplation can represent almost a flight from ourselves or from reality, a neurotic wanderlust that generates lives of haste and impermanence.

Precisely in this context, "often in a confused way, a unique and growing demand for spirituality and for the supernatural does not fail to re-emerge. This is a sign of anxiety which dwells in the hearts of people who are not open to the transcendent horizon of God. . . . Unfortunately it is God himself who is excluded from the horizon of so many people; and when the topic of God does not meet with indifference, closure or rejection, people wish in any case to relegate it to the subjective context, reducing it to an intimate and private factor, marginalised from public awareness".[10]

4. Consecrated life, characterised by the constant search for God and by the continual revisiting of his identity, is surrounded by the demands and cultural climate of this world which, having lost the awareness of God and of his effective presence in history, runs the risk of not recognising itself. It is living in a time not only of *dis-enchantment*, *dis-cord*, and *in-difference*, but even of *non-sense*. For many it is a time of *disorientation*, of becoming so overwhelmed as to give up searching for the meaning of things, of becoming true castaways of the spirit.

In this time the Church - and consecrated life within it - is called to testify that "God exists. He is real, he is personal, he is provident, he is infinitely good; our creator, our truth, our happiness, to the point that this effort of fixing the gaze and the heart upon him, which we call

---

[10] Benedict XVI, address to the General Assembly of the Italian Episcopal Conference, Vatican City, 24th May 2012.

contemplation, becomes the highest and fullest act of the spirit, the act that still today can and must give pattern to the immense pyramid of human activity."[11]

This is the task entrusted to consecrated life: to witness, in our time, that God is happiness. Fixing our gaze and our heart on him allows us to live in fulness.

The term "contemplate" is used in everyday language to indicate prolonged gazing, attentive observation of something that prompts wonder or admiration: the spectacle of nature, the starry sky, a painting, a monument, the landscape. This gaze, in grasping beauty and savouring it, can go beyond whatever is being contemplated, and set out in search of the author of beauty (cf. *Wis* 13:1-9; *Rom* 1:20). It is a gaze that contains within itself something that goes beyond the eyes: the gaze of a mother upon the child sleeping in her arms, or the gaze of an elderly couple who, after a life lived together, persevere in their love. It is a gaze that communicates intensely, expresses a relationship, recounts what it is that I am for someone else.

Now, since it is true that the origin of the term "contemplation" is Greek (*theorein/theoria*), and the word indicates an intuition of the reason which, from the multiplicity of whatever is seen, reascends to the one, and grasps the whole through these fragments and the ultimate nature of things through the phenomena, then it is even more true that biblical man has an essentially contemplative *animus*. In his amazement as a creature, aware of receiving being and existence from a free and gratuitous act of God, he finds the resolution of every anxiety of his heart. The *Psalms* are imbued with this gaze of gratitude and wonder upon man and things.

5. Biblical man is aware of the loving initiative and liberality of God in another area as well: the gift of the Word. God's initiative toward his creature, woven together with him in dialogue, and ushering him into that personal relationship which is covenant - I for you and you for me - is not a "given", not something we should take for granted. It is a surprising revelation before which we should simply "stand" in an attitude of receptivity and gratitude.

---

[11] Paul VI, allocution on the occasion of the last public session of the Second Vatican Council, 7th December 1965.

The prophets are qualified witnesses of this attitude. The *ten words* with which the covenant is sealed (cf. *Ex* 34:28) are introduced with *Hear, O Israel* (*Dt* 6:4). The first sin, or better, the root of every sin for Israel, is forgetfulness of the Word: so it is in the beginning, with the claim of autonomy from God (cf. *Gen* 3:3-6), and so, in a severe reproof of the people, Moses and the prophets denounce the forsaking of the covenant. "The word of God also inevitably reveals the tragic possibility that human freedom can withdraw from this covenant dialogue with God for which we were created. The divine word also discloses the sin that lurks in the human heart".[12]

In the fulness of time, God's initiative reaches its completion: the Word has been condensed to the point of becoming flesh and dwelling among us, has been abbreviated to the point of remaining silent in the decisive *hour* of the Passion: the creation gives way to redemption, which is the new creation.

The term "contemplation" is found only once in the New Testament. The only text that uses the terminology of contemplation refers to the human gaze and heart fixed on Jesus Christ crucified, on him who told men about God (cf. *Jn* 1:18). The moment selected comes immediately after Jesus's death, with the exclamation of the centurion who, beneath the cross, proclaims: Truly this was a just man! (*Lk* 23:47). Luke notes: *The whole crowd that had come to see this spectacle* (Greek: *theoría*; Latin: *spectaculum*) *went away thinking about what had happened and beating their breasts* (*Lk* 23:48). The passage from Luke speaks of unity between exteriority and interiority, of gazing and repentance. The act of seeing and the gesture of beating the breast indicate a deep unity within the person, a unity that is created mysteriously before Christ. The term *theoría* (contemplation) therefore designates the "*concrete spectacle. . . of Jesus of Nazareth, the crucified 'King of the Jews'*".[13]

Contemplation is therefore "a gaze of faith, fixed on Jesus";[14] according to the simple words of the peasant of Ars to his saintly parish priest, "I

---

[12] Benedict XVI, post-synodal apostolic exhortation *Verbum Domini* (30th September 2010), 26. Among the biblical texts can be cited, for example: *Dt* 28:1-2,15,45; 32:1; among the prophets cf. *Jer* 7:22-28; *Ez* 2:8; 3:10; 6:3; 13:2; up to the end: cf. *Zec* 3:8. For St Paul cf. *Rm* 10:14-18; 1 *Thess* 2:13.

[13] G. Dossetti, *"L'esperienza religiosa. Testimonianza di un monaco"*, in AA.VV., *L'esperienza religiosa oggi* (Milan, Vita e Pensiero, 1986), 223.

[14] *Catechism of the Catholic Church*, no. 2715.

look at him and he looks at me".[15] St Teresa of Jesus, in the same way, explains: "Just as here below, if two persons love each other very much and are mentally alert, even without any sign it seems that they understand each other with only a look, so it must be in such a circumstance in which, although we cannot understand how, these two lovers gaze intently at each other; in the same way in which the bridegroom speaks to the bride in the *Song of Songs*, according to what I seem to have understood, this is what happens here".[16]

Contemplation is therefore the gaze of man upon God and *upon the works of his hands* (cf. *Ps* 8:4). It is, to return to the words of Blessed Paul VI, "the effort of fixing the gaze and the heart upon Him. . . the highest and fullest act of the spirit".[17]

6. Consecrated persons are called, perhaps now more than ever, to be prophets, mystics, and contemplatives, to discover the signs of God's presence in everyday life, to become wise interlocutors who are able to recognise the questions that God and humanity pose in the wake of our history. The great challenge is the capacity to "continue to 'see' God with the eyes of faith in a world which ignores his presence".[18]

Life itself, just as it is, is called to become the place of our contemplation. Cultivating the interior life need not generate an existence between heaven and earth, in ecstasy and illumination, but a life that in humble closeness to God and in sincere empathy creates and realises within history a purified and transfigured existence.

Dietrich Bonhoeffer uses the image of the *cantus firmus*[19] to explain how the encounter with God allows the believer to contemplate the world, human beings, and the tasks to be performed, with a contemplative attitude; and this attitude permits him to see, live, and taste in all things the mysterious presence of the Triune God.

---

[15] Ibid.

[16] St Teresa of Avila, *Book of Life*, 27, 10.

[17] Paul VI, allocution on the occasion of the last public session of the Second Vatican, 7th December 1965.

[18] John Paul II, post-synodal apostolic exhortation *Vita Consecrata* (25th March 1996), 68.

[19] Dietrich Bonhoeffer, *Lettera a Renata ed Eberhard Bethge*, in *Opere di Dietrich Bonhoeffer*, v. 8: *Resistenza e resa* (Brescia, Queriniana, 2002), 412.

The contemplative unites little by little, through a long process, his work for God with the sensitivity to perceive him, hears the sounds of God's footsteps in the events of everyday life, becomes an expert in the *murmuring of a gentle breeze (1 K* 19:12) of that everyday life in which the Lord makes himself present.

In the Church the contemplative and active dimensions are interwoven in such a way that they cannot be separated. The constitution *Sacrosanctum Concilium* emphasises the theandric nature of the Church, which is "both human and divine, visible but endowed with invisible realities, eager to act and yet intent on contemplation, present in this world and yet not at home in it; and she is all these things in such wise that in her the human is directed and subordinated to the divine, the visible likewise to the invisible, action to contemplation, and this present world to that city yet to come, which we seek".[20]

Let us return to the beginning and foundation of our whole life: the relationship with the Mystery of the living God, the primacy of life in the Spirit, the communion of love with Jesus, "the centre of [our] life and the continual source of every initiative",[21] an experience we are called to share.[22]

We, the consecrated, would do well to remember that no ecclesial action can bear fruit for the Gospel without *remaining* intimately united with Christ, who is Life (cf. *Jn* 15:1-11): *Without me you can do nothing* (*Jn* 15:5). He who does not remain in Christ can give nothing to the world, can do nothing to transform the structures of sin. He will exert himself in many things, important perhaps but not essential (cf. *Lk* 10:38-42), with the risk of running in vain.

Pope Francis encourages us: "Jesus wants evangelisers who proclaim the good news not only with words, but above all by a life transfigured by God's presence... Spirit-filled evangelisers are evangelisers who pray and work... What is needed is the ability to cultivate an interior space which can give a Christian meaning to commitment and activity. Without

---

[20] Second Vatican Council, constitution on the sacred liturgy *Sacrosanctum Concilium*, 2.

[21] Congregation for Institutes of Consecrated Life and Societies of Apostolic Life, instruction *Starting Afresh From Christ: A Renewed Commitment to Consecrated Life in the Third Millennium* (19th May 2002), 22.

[22] John Paul II, post-synodal apostolic exhortation *Vita Consecrata* (25th March 1996), 16.

prolonged moments of adoration, of prayerful encounter with the word, of sincere conversation with the Lord, our work easily becomes meaningless; we lose energy as a result of weariness and difficulties, and our fervour dies out. The Church urgently needs the deep breath of prayer".[23]

7. In the Church, as *cantus firmus, exclusively contemplative* brothers and sisters are "a sign of the exclusive union of the Church as Bride with her Lord, whom she loves above all things",[24] but this letter is not dedicated exclusively to them. We call for a shared exploration of the contemplative dimension in the heart of the world, the foundation of all consecrated life and the true source of ecclesial fruitfulness. Contemplation asks the consecrated person to go forward in new methods of the spirit:

- A new way of standing in relationship with God, with oneself, with others, with created things, which are *bearers of meaning* about him.[25] The contemplative person crosses barriers until he reaches the source, which is God; he opens the eyes of his heart in order to be able to *look at, consider, and contemplate* the presence of God in persons, in history, and in events.

- A personal encounter with the God of history, who in the person of his Son *came to dwell among us* (cf. *Jn* 1:14), and makes himself present in the history of each person, in everyday events, and in the wonderful work of creation. The contemplative person does not see life as an obstacle, but as a mirror that mystically reflects the *Mirror*.[26]

- An experience of faith that is more than just the vocal confession of the creed, allowing the truth contained in it to become the practice of life. The contemplative person is above all a believing person, a person of faith, with an *incarnate faith* and not a purely theoretical faith (a "*laboratory faith*").[27]

---

[23] Pope Francis, apostolic exhortation *Evangelii Gaudium* (24th November 2013), 259; 262.

[24] John Paul II, post-synodal apostolic exhortation *Vita Consecrata* (25th March 1996), 59.

[25] St Francis of Assisi, *Canticle of the Creatures*, 4.

[26] Cf. St Clare, *Fourth letter to Blessed Agnes of Prague*, in *FF* [*Fonti Francescani*], 2901-2903.

[27] Antonio Spadaro, *Interview with Pope Francis* (Italian text in *La Civiltà Cattolica*, 164 (2013/III), 474).

- A *relationship of friendship*, a *tratar de amistad*,[28] as affirmed by the first female doctor of the Church, St Teresa of Jesus; the gift of a God who desires to communicate deeply with man, as a true friend (cf. *Jn* 15:15). To contemplate is to enjoy the friendship of the Lord, in the intimacy of a Friend.

- An immersion in the impassioned search for a God who dwells within us and is always setting out on the road in search of man. The contemplative person understands that the personal ego marks the distance between God and himself, and because of this, he does not cease to be a *beggar* for the Beloved, seeking him in the right place, in the depths of the self, the shrine where God dwells.

- An openness to the revelation and communion of the living God through Christ in the Holy Spirit.[29] The contemplative person allows himself to be filled with revelation and transformed by communion, becomes a luminous icon of the Trinity, and presents amid human frailty "the attraction of divine beauty".[30] All of this happens in the silence of life, where words are hushed in such a way that the gaze may speak, full of the childlike wonder; so that what speaks may be open hands, hands that share in the gesture of the mother who expects nothing in return; and so that what speaks may be the feet of the *messenger* (*Is* 52:7), capable of crossing borders for the sake of proclaiming the Gospel.

Contemplation therefore does not justify a mediocre, repetitive, boring life. "God alone is enough" for those who follow Jesus: he is the intrinsic and indispensable dimension of this choice. The contemplatives and mystics of Christian history have walked with "hearts set on the Lord".[31] For consecrated persons, following Jesus is always a *contemplative discipleship* and contemplation is the fulness of a *discipleship* that transfigures.

---

[28] St Teresa of Avila, *Life* 8, 5.

[29] Cf. Congregation for Institutes of Consecrated Life and Societies of Apostolic Life, *The contemplative dimension of religious life* (Plenary, March 1980), 1.

[30] John Paul II, post-synodal apostolic exhortation *Vita Consecrata* (25th March 1996), 20.

[31] Cf. St Francis of Assisi, *Rule*, 19.25.

SEEKING

Have you seen him whom my soul loves?
(Song of Songs, 3:3)

LISTENING

8. To love means to declare oneself ready to live a daily apprenticeship of seeking. The dynamics of the search witness that no one is sufficient for himself; they demand that he set out on an exodus within his own depths, attracted by that "sacred land which is the other",[32] in order to be incorporated into communion. The other is, however, a mystery, always beyond our desires and expectations, is not predictable, does not ask to be possessed but for care, protection, and room to flourish in freedom. If this is true of the human creature, how much more so is it of God, the mystery of supreme freedom, of dynamic relationship, of a fulness whose greatness surpasses us, whose weakness - manifested through the cross - disarms us.

Love, in the *Song*, is struggle and effort, just like death (*māwet*, *Song* 8:6) It is not idealised, but sung of in full awareness of its crises and confusions. The search involves effort, it requires us to rise and set out on the journey; it requires us to accept the darkness of the "night". The night is the absence, separation, or removal of *him whom the heart loves*, and the bridal chamber, instead of being a place of rest and dreams, turns into a prison and a place of nightmares and torments (cf. *Song* 3:1). The bride, who is the main character of the drama, seeks the beloved, but he is absent. It is necessary to seek him, to go out *through the streets and through the squares* (*Song* 3:2). Defying the dangers of the night, devoured by the desire to embrace him again, the bride poses the eternal question: *Have you seen him whom my heart loves*? (*Song* 3:2). It is a question cried aloud in the heart of the night, that evokes the joy of his memory, and renews the wound of an unbearable separation. The bride is sleepless.

The night comes back to the forefront in chapter five of the *Song*: the young woman is in her chamber, her beloved knocks and asks to enter, but she hesitates and he goes away (*Song* 5:2-6). Is this a dynamic of incomprehension between the two of them, or a dream that turns into a terrible nightmare? The text continues with a new search that has the flavour of a great trial, not only emotional and affective but also physical,

---

[32] Cf. Pope Francis, apostolic exhortation *Evangelii Gaudium* (24th November 2013), 169.

because the bride who faces the night alone is struck by the guards, wounded and deprived of her cloak (*Song* 5:7). Love defies the night and its dangers; it is greater than any fear: *In love there is no fear, but perfect love casts out fear* (*1 Jn* 4:18).

In seeking the bridegroom, the woman demonstrates an understanding of her interior condition. She examines her depths and finds that she is *sick with love* (*Song* 2:5; 5:8). This illness is called the "alteration" of one's proper condition, because by virtue of the encounter with the beloved one feels irreversibly marked, "altered"; one feels one has become "other", chosen, consecrated to another, who fills one's days with meaning. This is the condition of anyone who truly loves.

Only one who overcomes the travail of the night with the name of the beloved on her lips and his face impressed upon her heart, certain of the bond that unites them, can taste the fresh joy of encounter. The fire of love sets up a heartbreaking relationship between the two lovers; having emerged from the winter of solitude, they taste the springtime of communion and compete to outdo each other in celebrating the other's beauty with passion and poetry.

THE EVERYDAY APPRENTICESHIP OF SEEKING

9. "*Faciem tuam, Domine, requiram*: your face, O Lord, I seek (*Ps* 26:8). A pilgrim in search of the meaning of life, enveloped in the great mystery that surrounds him, man in fact seeks, even if often unconsciously, the Lord's face. *Lord, make me know your ways, teach me your paths* (*Ps* 24:4): no one can ever take from the heart of the human person the search for him of whom the Bible says he is all (*Eccl* 43:27) and for the ways to reach him".[33]

The search for God unites all men of good will, and even those who profess themselves to be nonbelievers confess this profound yearning of the heart.

---

[33] Congregation for Institutes of Consecrated Life and Societies of Apostolic Life, instruction *The service of authority and obedience*: *Faciem tuam, Domine, requiram* (11th May 2008), 1.

On various occasions Pope Francis has described the contemplative dimension of life as entering into the mystery. "'To enter into the mystery' means the ability to wonder, to contemplate; the ability to listen to the silence and to hear the tiny whisper amid great silence by which God speaks to us. To enter into the mystery demands that we not be afraid of reality: that we not be locked into ourselves, that we not flee from what we fail to understand, that we not close our eyes to problems or deny them, that we not dismiss our questions. . . To enter into the mystery means going beyond our own comfort zone, beyond the laziness and indifference which hold us back, and going out in search of truth, beauty and love. It is seeking a deeper meaning, an answer, and not an easy one, to the questions which challenge our faith, our fidelity and our very existence."[34]

10. Entering into the mystery involves a continual search, the necessity of going beyond, of not closing one's eyes, of seeking answers. Human beings are in constant tension towards improvement, continually on a journey, on a quest. Living in permanent dissatisfaction, anaesthetised by powerful emotions, is a constant risk. This is why ours is a time of failure and of downfall, of indifference and the loss of taste. It is essential to be aware of this consuming unease, an unease that intercepts the sounds of the postmodern soul and reawakens amid fragility vigorous roots, so as to make known to the world the prophetic vitality of the Gospel.

The Christian life "demands and entails a transformation, a purification, a moral and spiritual elevation of man; that is, it demands the search, the true striving for a personal condition, an interior state of sentiments, of thoughts, of mentality and an exterior state of conduct, and a richness of grace and gifts that we call perfection".[35] In our rush towards goals of chance, consumption, fashion, power, whim, driven by repetitive compulsions, we are looking for new forms of enjoyment, but are never satisfied: in our day men and women, in this search for the illusory, gain only a sense of despair that closes off life and extinguishes it.

St Augustine made a diagnosis, pointing out that people are not always able to make the qualitative leap that drives them to go beyond, to seek the infinite, because "they adapt themselves to what they can do and they

---

[34] Pope Francis, *Homily for the Easter Vigil*, Vatican basilica (Saturday, 4th April 2015).
[35] Paul VI, general audience, Vatican City, 7th August 1968.

are satisfied with this, because that which they cannot do they do not desire enough to attain it".[36]

In this fog of conscience and the affections, the sometimes tragic experience of today reawakens the need for the liberating encounter with the living God; we are called to be wise and patient mouthpieces for these inexpressible groanings (cf. *Rm* 8:26-27) so that the yearning for God may not be extinguished, but kept glowing beneath the ashes of indifference.

Faced with this re-emergence of the search for the sacred, we cannot ignore how - even among those who profess themselves to be Christians - faith appears to be reduced to brief religious parentheses, which do not touch everyday problems. Faith becomes extraneous to life. God is not necessary, he is not part of life, as family, friends, tender affections, work, home or finances are. This extraneousness can also affect our consecrated life.

PILGRIMS TO THE CORE

11. "If man is essentially a wayfarer, this means that he is on a journey toward a destination that we can call at the same time, and contradictorily, both seen and unseen. But restlessness is precisely, as it were, the inner spring of this progress"[37] even in a time of technological power and its ideals, and "man cannot lose this spur without becoming immobile and without dying".[38]

It is God alone who reawakens the restlessness and power of our questioning, the insomnia that makes us get up and set out. This is the driving power of the journey: restlessness before the questions raised by life drives man on his questing pilgrimage.

At the root of Christian life is the fundamental movement of faith: to set off toward Jesus in order to centre one's life on him. This exodus leads to knowing God and his love. It is a pilgrimage that knows its destination, a radical change that turns nomads into pilgrims. Being pilgrims involves movement, activity, engagement. The path we must take implies risk, insecurity, openness to new things and to unexpected encounters.

---

[36] St Augustine, *Confessions* X.xxiii.33.
[37] Gabriel Marcel, *Homo viator. Prolégomènes à une métaphysique de l'espérance* (Paris, Aubier, 1944), 26.
[38] Ibid.

A pilgrim is not simply someone who goes from one place to another. He does not put off the search for the destination; he knows where he wants to go, he has a goal that calls to his heart and tenaciously pushes his steps onwards. He does not just nourish a vague search for happiness, but looks to a precise goal, which he knows or at least glimpses, a goal about which he has news and for which he has decided to depart. The destination of the Christian is God.

QUAERERE DEUM

12. St Benedict, that tenacious seeker of God, insists that the monk is not one who has found God: he is one who seeks him throughout his life. In the *Rule*, he calls for an examination of the motivations of the young monk for the sake of verifying in the first place *"si revera Deum quaerit"*, if he truly seeks God.[39]

This is the paradigm of the life of every Christian, of every consecrated person: the search for God, *si revera Deum quaerit*. The Latin word *quaerere* does not mean only to seek, to go in search of something, to strive to attain it, but also to ask, to pose a question. The human being is one who asks and seeks incessantly. To seek God, therefore, means never becoming weary of asking, like the bride of the *Song*: *Have you seen him whom my soul loves?* (*Song* 3:3).

The narrative thread of the *Song* is represented precisely by the theme of the lover's search, of the presence savoured after bitter absence, of dawn welcomed after the night, of forgetfulness of self lived as a condition for finding the Other.

The first level of love is that of the love that seeks. Desire and seeking are the dominant experiences, and the Other is perceived as the absent Presence. The spouses of the *Song* are presented as beggars for love, ardent seekers of the beloved.

Seeking God means entering into relationship with him and allowing this Presence to engage our humanity. This means never being satisfied with what we have attained. God incessantly asks us: *Where are you?* (*Gen* 3:9). The search for God demands humility: our truth is revealed by the light of the Spirit and in this we recognise that it is God who seeks us first.

---

[39] St Benedict, *Rule*, 58, 7.

"The restless heart of which we spoke earlier, echoing St Augustine, is the heart that is ultimately satisfied with nothing less than God, and in this way becomes a loving heart. . . . But not only are we restless for God: God's heart is restless for us. God is waiting for us. He is looking for us. He knows no rest either, until he finds us. God's heart is restless, and that is why he set out on the path towards us - to Bethlehem, to Calvary, from Jerusalem to Galilee and on to the very ends of the earth. God is restless for us, he looks out for people willing to 'catch' his unrest, his passion for us, people who carry within them the searching of their own hearts and at the same time open themselves to be touched by God's search for us".[40]

The reason for our search leads back to the Love that was the first to seek us and touch us, while we recognise its seal. It can happen that refusing to search may silence the voice within us that calls us to completion. It can happen that we stop to enjoy the illusory glamours, satisfied with bread that assuages hunger for a day, repeating for ourselves the initial choice of the *prodigal son* (cf. *Lk* 15:11-32).

Sometimes, the horizon becomes narrowed, and the heart no longer waits for *him who comes*. But God always comes so that the primacy of Love may be established in our life. There is a return to the dynamic of the *Song*, the game of searching: we cannot imagine finding God once and for all.

THE SEARCH IN THE NIGHT

13. *Upon my bed by night I sought him whom my soul loves; I sought him, but found him not; I called him, but he gave no answer* (*Song* 3:1). The reading of the *Song* envelops one in the idyll of a dreamlike love, while it introduces the recurrent and vivid suffering of the enamoured soul. Love, an experience that transforms and not an ephemeral and brief encounter, calls us to live with the possibility that the beloved will be absent, and at times we may experience exile, rupture, or separation. This possibility gives rise to anticipation, to reciprocal and constant search: a cry of the soul that is never satisfied. The *Song* places us before a time of crisis, of

---

[40] Benedict XVI, *Homily* on the occasion of the Solemnity of the Epiphany of the Lord, Vatican basilica, 6th January 2012.

encounter, the moment, after the initial fire and passion, in which one is recognised and accepted. It is the moment of loving in a different way. Separation becomes search, while the yearning that rends and wounds becomes the necessary food of love.

DESIRE

14. Love for God necessarily maintains this attitude of desire. God is invisible, he is always beyond everything, our search for him is never fulfilled. His is an elusive presence: "God is he who seeks us and at the same time he who makes himself sought. He is the one who reveals himself and at the same time the one who conceals himself. He is the one spoken of in the words of the psalm: *Your face, O Lord, I seek* (*Ps* 26:8), and many other words of the Bible, like those of the bride in the *Song*: *Upon my bed by night I sought him whom my soul loves; I sought him, but found him not; I called him, but he gave no answer. I will rise now and go about the city, in the streets and in the squares; I will seek him whom my soul loves. I sought him, but found him not* (3:1-4)... Urged by the words of the *Song I sought him but found him not*, we confront the problem of atheism, or better, of ignorance about God. None of us is far from such experience: there is in us a potential atheist who cries out and murmurs every day his difficulties in believing".[41]

"*Si comprehendis, non est Deus*"[42] Augustine writes: that is, "if you think you have understood him, that is no longer God". The category of the search safeguards the distance between the seeking creature and the Creator: an essential distance because the Sought is not an object, but himself a subject, or rather the true subject, in that he is the one who first sought, called, and loved us, evoking the desire within our hearts.

Our search must be a humble one, because we recognise in ourselves "potential atheists"; we experience difficulty in believing. We recognise in ourselves that self-sufficient and at times arrogant pride which separates us from others and condemns us. Seeking God requires us to go through the night and even remain within it for a long time. It requires us to discover the power and beauty of a journey of faith that is able to confront the obscurity of doubt without presuming to offer solutions at

---

[41] C. M. Martini, *La tentazione dell'ateismo*, in *Il Corriere della Sera*, 16th November 2007.
[42] St Augustine, *Sermo* 52, 16.

any price. Lived faith will allow us to bear witness to Christ in the humble language of those who have learned how to dwell within the night and to live through its questions.

The night, in Scripture, is the time of travail, of interior struggle and spiritual combat, as with Jacob at the Jabbok (*Gen* 32:25). It is night when Nicodemus approaches Jesus, in secret for fear of the Jews (*Jn* 3:2); it is night when Judas becomes lost and separates himself from the vital friendship with Christ in leaving the upper room (*Jn* 13:30); it is still night when Mary Magdalen goes to the tomb (*Jn* 20:1) and is able to recognise the voice of the Beloved (cf. *Jn* 20:11-18), like the bride of the *Song* (*Song* 2:8). The night is a time of desire that turns into encounter if one goes through it without coming to doubt love.

Humble faith accepts that the dark passage toward the dawn does not stand for a passage from search to possession, but leads from the fragmentation that scatters the spirit to the unifying experience of the Risen One. Life takes on direction and meaning, while day after day, prayer after prayer, trial after trial, we make our pilgrimage towards the definitive answer, towards repose and quiet, towards peace of soul.

In our time, marked by fragility and insecurity, contemplation might be sought without any root in faith, solely as a "place" of quiet, of repose, as an emotional space, as the reward for a search for self that avoids effort and suffering. The Word of God, and the interpretation of certain experiences of holiness imbued with suffering or with the "night of faith", help us to avoid the temptation to escape the hardships of the human journey.

HOPE

15. The night, a dark and obscure symbol, becomes an image full of hope within biblical and Christian spirituality. The story of the Spirit is interwoven with the night that precedes the radiant and splendid day, the day of light. Passing through the dark night is marked by the crumbling of security in order to be born to new life. One reaches the light by passing through the darkness, to life through death, to day through night: this requires the life of faith. It is a time in which the person is called to dwell in God; the time in which those who are seeking are called to pass from the experience of being loved by God to that of loving God simply because he is God.

St John of the Cross has called the spiritual experience in which there is an alternation of disorientation, aridity, powerlessness, pain, and desperation, the *dark night*; a night of the spirit and of the senses, a passage toward the perfect union of love with God. Teresa of Avila, at the height of her reform activity with the Carmelites, tells it like this: "So then," she recounts in her *Life*, "I forgot about the graces received, of which there remained to me only a memory like a faraway dream that added to my suffering. My intelligence was obfuscated and I found myself wrapped in a thousand doubts and anxieties. It seemed that I could not really grasp what was happening in me, and I wondered if this was nothing more than a matter of my own imagination. And so I thought: why should I deceive others as well? Wasn't it enough for me to be deceived on my own? And in the meantime I became so pessimistic as to believe that all the evils and heresies that were devastating the world were the effect of my sins".[43]

There are many such examples, from Francis of Assisi to Thérèse of Lisieux, from Gemma Galgani to Bernadette Soubirous, from Padre Pio to Teresa of Calcutta, who writes: "There is so much contradiction in my soul, a profound yearning for God, so profound as to hurt, a continual suffering - and with this the sentiment of not being wanted by God, rejected, empty, without faith, without love, without zeal. Heaven means nothing to me, it appears to me an empty place".[44] The darkness becomes a proving ground for love, fidelity, and the mysterious nearness of God.

O vere beata nox, "O truly blessed night",[45] we sing at the Easter Vigil, and proclaim the resurrection and victory. The night becomes a time and way for the coming of the Bridegroom who unites to himself and with his embrace transforms the soul, as the Spanish mystic sings:

O night that guided me,
O night more pleasing than the dawn!
O night that reunited
the lover with the beloved,
the beloved in the lover transformed![46]

---

[43] St Teresa of Avila, *Vita*, 30, 8.

[44] Blessed Teresa of Calcutta, *Come be my light*, edited by B. Kolodiejchuk, (New York, Doubleday, 2007).

[45] Roman Missal, Easter Proclamation (the Exsultet).

[46] St John of the Cross, *Poems*, V, 'The dark night', 5-8.

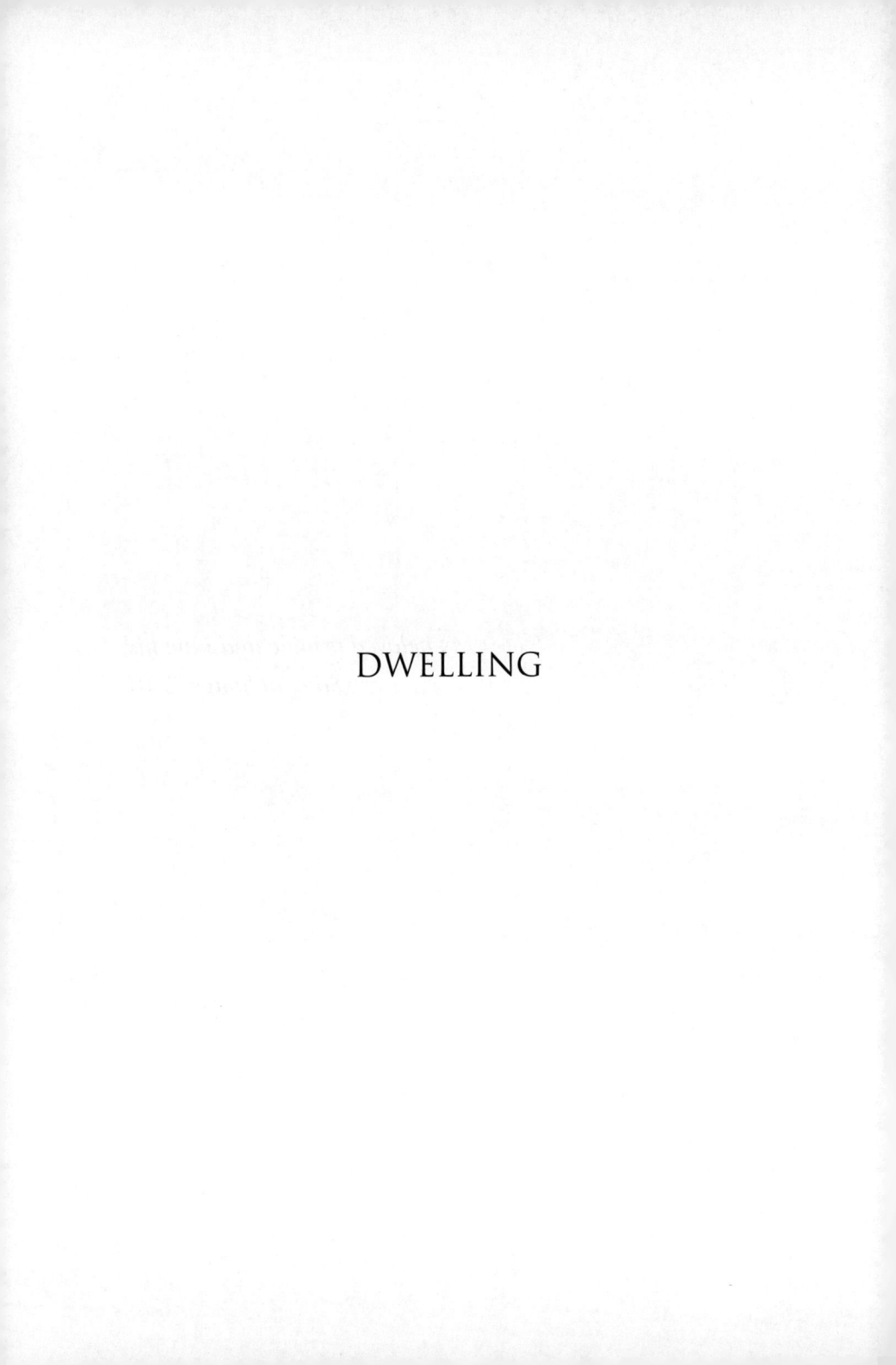

DWELLING

My beloved is mine and I am his.
(Song of Songs, 2:16)

LISTENING

16. The *Song* unfurls along the line of seeking and finding, in a harmonious epiphany of encounter and of mutual contemplation according to a very precise linguistic register: that of *praise*. Praise involves the whole body, the concrete place of relationship with the other: lips, teeth, cheeks, neck, hair, breasts, hands, legs, and in particular the eyes, which launch signals of love that are compared to doves (*Song* 1:15; 4:1; 5:12).

The fulness of the heart is expressed through the celebratory language of the body. Praise of bodily beauty is expressed through the language of nature, of building, of goldsmithing, of the emotions. The universe coalesces in the body of the one who loves, and the loved one appears present in the universe. The word is consecrated to love and the language of communion is used. Love becomes a continual and lively dialogue that grasps beauty and celebrates it. The praise of the bridegroom: *How beautiful you are, my beloved, how beautiful you are!* (*Song* 1:15), is followed by that of the bride: *How handsome you are, my beloved, how gracious!* (*Song* 1:16). These "fair-spoken" words heal the wounds inflicted by the language of accusation, evident in the relationship between man and woman after original sin (cf. *Gen* 3:12) and permit the restoration of equality, reciprocity, and mutual belonging: *My beloved is mine and I am his* (*Song* 2:16), *I am my beloved's and my beloved is mine* (*Song* 6:3), *I am my beloved's and his desire is for me* (*Song* 7:11), an expression that seems to put an end to the divine punishment expressed in *Genesis* (3:16). The language of praise and compliment brings about a relational harmony that is also reflected in creation, which is never separated from human affairs (cf. *Rm* 8:22-23) and is harmonised with the human heart in celebration through an abundance of colours, scents, flavours and sounds.

Even God, fascinated with his creature, showers it with compliments, as he does with Mary when he greets her with the title *full of grace* (*kecharitoméne*, *Lk* 1:28), thus proclaiming her to be a masterpiece of beauty. The creature responds with the *Magnificat* (*Lk* 1:46-55), placing within the story the power of praise that swells the human heart and ushers it into an authentic relationship with God.

17. The word that leaps forth to set love free reaches for contact, for union. The *Song* opens with the plea that issues from the lips of the bride, the main character of the drama, and manifests her desire for contact with the beloved, physically absent but present in her heart and in her thoughts. His mouth becomes a spring from which she can draw to quench her thirst and make herself drunk: *May he kiss me with the kisses of his mouth! For your love is better than wine , your anointing oils are fragrant, your name is oil poured out; therefore the maidens love you* (Song 1:2-3). The kisses and tenderness of the Bridegroom (*dodîm*) are described as *tôbîm* (good), meaning that they present the proper characteristic of all that comes from the hands of the Creator (cf. *Gen* 1:4), in keeping with the original divine plan. They represent a *liturgy of communion*, access to one another's breathing, a joy greater than the thrill that is given by wine: *we will rejoice and be glad in you, we will remember your love more than wine* (Song 1:4). The beloved cannot be resisted, because love is a reality so inescapable and strong as to be comparable only to *death* (*Song* 8:6); it is a reality with an incredible attractive force that leads the two to become one.

18. This applies both to conjugal life (cf. *Gen* 2:24) and to consecrated life, which lives, in an analogous way, the dynamism of spousal love with Christ (cf. *1 Cor* 6:17). It flourishes, in fact, within love, a love that fascinates, engages the deepest desires, touches the wellsprings, and prompts the desire to give. It is born as a response of love to a God who gives himself without reserve, a response to a gratuitous love that cannot be possessed, but only received. "This love embraces the whole person, soul and body, whether man or woman, in that person's unique and unrepeatable personal 'I'. The One who, given eternally to the Father, 'gives' himself in the mystery of the Redemption, has now called man in order that he in his turn should give himself entirely to the work of the Redemption through membership in a community of brothers or sisters, recognised and approved by the Church".[47]

---

[47] John Paul II, apostolic exhortation *Redemptionis donum* (25th March 1984), 3.

This dynamic of search and connection is a journey that is never fully completed. The person called is set upon a way of conversion and prayer in which to live. In these, desire becomes transformation and purification, praise and pattern, in a Beauty that attracts and unites: a mystery in which to live. "This intimate and profound knowledge of Christ is actuated and grows deeper day by day through the life of personal, community and liturgical prayer".[48]

IN THE FORM OF BEAUTY

19. At the heart of the Christian identity, as the power that moulds and shapes it, stands the revelation of God, as creation and salvation, a splendour that appeared once and for all in Christ and in his Passion. In the Son and in his earthly life God realises the intention of making himself known and of revealing the creature to itself: "We are marked by God in the Spirit. Just as in fact we die in Christ to be reborn, so also we are marked by the Spirit so as to be able to bear his splendour, image, and grace".[49] There echoes the reciprocal recognition of beginnings. God expresses his satisfaction to the human creature: *He saw what he had made, and behold, it was very good* (*Gen* 1:31). He binds him to himself with a love that, in recognition, restores him to beauty: *How beautiful you are, my beloved, how beautiful you are* (*Song* 1:15); a love that is absolute and inextinguishable: *I am my beloved's and his desire is for me* (*Song* 7:11).

Let us hold our contemplative gaze upon the mystery of the Beauty, of which we are a form. The traditions of both the West and the East introduce us and enlighten us on the Christian form of beauty, its unicity, its ultimate significance. In the heartbreaking exclamation of the *Confessions*: "Late have I loved you, beauty ever ancient and ever new!",[50] we find the cry of the human soul at all times. The necessity of a journey, leading from beauty to Beauty, sounds clearly; a journey from the penultimate to the Ultimate, to find in the foundation of all beauty the meaning and measure

---

[48] Ibid., 8.
[49] St Ambrose, *The Holy Spirit*, I, 6, 79.
[50] St Augustine, *Confessions*, X, 27, 38.

of all that exists: "Behold, you were within me, I was outside: here I sought you and, deformed as I was, I threw myself upon the beautiful things that you have made. . . You called, you cried, you overcame my deafness; you blazed, you shone, and you dispelled my blindness".[51]

20. The Church, when singing Vespers during the season of Lent and Holy Week, introduces *Psalm 44* with two texts of Scripture that seem to be in opposition. The first key of interpretation recognises Christ as the most handsome among men: *You are the most handsome among the sons of men, grace is poured out upon your lips* (*Ps* 44). The grace poured out upon his lips indicates the inner beauty of his word, the glory of the Truth, the beauty of God that attracts us to him and inflicts upon us the wound of Love. In the Bride-Church, he moves us toward the Love that has impressed its form on us. Let us live in the form of beauty, not as aesthetic nostalgia, but with primary reference to the love that dwells within us: *Your God will be your splendour* (*Is* 60:19; cf. *Wis* 8:2).

The second text of Scripture invites us to read the same psalm with a different interpretative key, this time from Isaiah: *He has no appearance or beauty to attract our gaze, no splendour that he might please us* (*Is* 53:2). How can this be reconciled? *The most handsome among men* is of such wretched appearance that there is no desire to look at him. Pilate presents him to the crowd saying: *Ecce homo*, so as to elicit pity for the disfigured and beaten man: a man without a face.

21. "A Jesus ugly and deformed? A Jesus more handsome and gracious than any other man? Yes, this is what two trumpets say that are played in different ways, but with the same Spirit blown into them. The first trumpet says: Handsome of face more than the sons of men; and the second, with Isaiah, says: We have seen him: he had no beauty, no majesty. . . Do not refuse to hear them together, seek instead to listen to them and understand them".[52] St Augustine reconciles the oppositions - not contradictions - by manifesting the splendour of true Beauty, Truth itself. He who believes in the God who has manifested himself as *love to the end* (*Jn* 13:1) in the tormented body of Christ crucified, knows that beauty is truth and

---
[51] Ibid.
[52] St Augustine, *Commentary on the first letter of John*, 9, 9.

truth is beauty. In the suffering Christ, however, he also learns that the beauty of the truth includes offence, suffering even as far as the obscure mystery of death. It is in the acceptance of suffering, and not in ignoring it, that our encounter with Beauty can take place, even when weak eyes or a heart wounded by evil are incapable of grasping its mysterious and fertile fabric.[53]

22. It is the incarnate Word who is the way of ultimate Beauty: "Our life has descended down here; he has taken hold of our death, has killed it with the superabundance of life. He has departed from our eyes so that we may enter within ourselves again and find him there".[54] The Word Jesus leads us to the source of beauty, attracts us with bonds of love: *How beautiful you are, my beloved, how gracious!* (*Song* 1:16). Beauty goes through a second passage: love in response. It moves, to encounter, to contemplate; it undertakes the journey, prompted by the love that has come to us as grace and freedom.

We are invited to the journey towards meeting and to living in it, while God restores our properly beautiful identity to us: *When Moses went down from Mount Sinai... he did not know that the skin of his face had become radiant, because he had spoken with him* (*Ex* 34:29).

23. The mystical tradition safeguards beauty in silence; it does not intend to violate it. The way of beauty requires exile, seclusion, unifying tension. It is the line that connects monastic theology with the great flowering of mysticism between the late Middle Ages and the dawn of the Modern Age.

The voice of Dionysius the Pseudo-Areopagite is heard: "Even in God *eros* is ecstatic, in that it never permits the lovers to belong to themselves, but only to the beloved... That is why the great Paul as well, entirely seized by divine *eros* and having become a participant in its ecstatic power, cries out in an inspired voice: 'It is no longer I who live, but Christ lives in me'. He is speaking as a true lover, as one who, according to his own words, has gone out from himself in ecstasy to enter into God, and

---

[53] Cf. J. Ratzinger, *La corrispondenza del cuore nell'incontro con la Bellezza*, in *30 Giorni*, no. 9, September 2002, 87.

[54] St Augustine, *Confessions*, IV, 12, 19.

no longer lives his own life, but that of the infinitely lovable beloved"[55]. Divinisation already begins on earth, the creature is transfigured and the kingdom of God is inaugurated: the splendour of God in the ecclesial form of the *ordo amoris* burns within the person as existence and a new way of life. *This life which I live in the body, I live in faith in the Son of God who loved me and gave himself up for me* (*Gal* 2:20).

24. Beauty is ecstatic. It can be reached only by one who loses himself, who agrees to make an interior journey that paradoxically leads outside his own ego in the movement of love: *My beloved is mine and I am his* (*Song* 2:16); *I am my beloved's and my beloved's is mine* (*Song* 6:3). The experience that brings us into relationship with the Lord, desired and sought, becomes the god-filled place in which the soul recognises itself and finds a dwelling: "My God, I contemplate you in the heaven of my soul, and I plunge into you".[56] In this abyss where everything resolves into unity and peace, God dwells mysterious and silent, the ineffable, the Other: "God from whom all that which is beautiful is beautiful and without whom nothing can be beautiful".[57]

St Maria Maddalena de' Pazzi describes the mystical experience that comes to know the splendour of God and of the creature seen in God: the soul united to the Word, *passus et gloriosus*, perceives the grafting of the human into the divine, absorbed into the trinitarian life, restored to the order of love.[58]

THE BEAUTY THAT WOUNDS

25. Beauty calls us to go out from ourselves, while its action of love opens in us the possibility of awareness, of enterprise, of vulnerability recognised and accepted.

Beauty strikes the human person, wounds him and precisely in this way gives him wings, raises him up with a desire so potent as to aspire to more than what it is fitting for man to aspire to: "These men have

---

[55] Ps-Dionysius the Areopagite, *De divinis nominibus* 4, 13.
[56] Blessed Elia di San Clemente, *Scritti* (Rome, 2006), 431.
[57] Cf. Achard of Saint Victor, *De unitate Dei et pluralitate creaturarum*, 1, 6.
[58] St Maria Maddalena de' Pazzi, *I colloqui*, parte seconda, in Tutte le opere, v. 3 (Florence, CIL, 1963), 226.

been struck by the Bridegroom himself; he himself has sent to their eyes an ardent ray of his beauty. The breadth of the wound already reveals what the arrow is like, and the intensity of the desire allows one to guess who it was who shot the bolt."[59] Thus Nicholas Kabasilas refers to the beauty that wounds, and in it he recognises both the presence of Christ and the *vulnus* that cries out within us as the desire for completion. This is a wound that calls us back to our ultimate destiny and to our mission. Pope Francis reminds us: "Whoever wants to preach must be the first to let the word of God move him deeply and become incarnate in his daily life. . . we need to let ourselves be penetrated by that word which will also penetrate others."[60]

26. In the journey that conforms us to the Son, we are invited to become aware of the possible deformation of the original image living in us, and of our vocation to be reborn from on high. This awareness must be lived in everyday life, taking on ourselves the risk of a demanding gaze that is not content with a restricted vision but trains itself to see and to manifest the graciousness of the Christian form. We are asked to train our gaze, to make it simple, purified, penetrating. We make a daily quest to live in the encounter, to recognise the habits that can distort it, and the laziness that can make us deaf: *A sound! The voice of my beloved who knocks: "Open to me, my sister, my friend. . ."* (*Song* 5:2).

The light of the Spirit comes to touch us in infinite ways, and his visit opens a wound in us, placing us in a state of passage. He urges us to make our own the demands and ways of the Beloved. He demolishes our securities. It is not easy to dwell amidst the detritus of all that grace has demolished. Temptation drives us to rebuild, to work. We consecrated men and women sometimes find in missionary activism a balm to soothe the wound created in us by grace. We glimpse the steps to be taken, but we stop there: *I have taken off my robe; how can I put it on again? I have washed my feet; how can I soil them again?* (*Song* 5:3). It is necessary to live with the wound, to abide in conversion.

---

[59] Nicholas Kabasilas, *La vita in Cristo* (Rome, Città Nuova, 1994), in J. Ratzinger, *La corrispondenza del cuore nell'incontro con la Bellezza*, in *30 Giorni*, no. 9, September 2002, 89.
[60] Pope Francis, apostolic exhortation *Evangelii Gaudium* (24th November 2013), 150.

27. The Spirit brings us into conversion (Greek *metanoeìn* = Hebrew *shub*), he capsizes us. The term *metanoeìn* emphasises this overturning and reveals that what is disrupted in us is the *nous*, the spiritual foundation, the innermost heart. Dwelling in conversion is a contemplative attitude, a surprise that is renewed every day and knows no end, in Christ Jesus.

Strangers to conversion, we become strangers to love. An invitation is called out to us consecrated men and women to the humility that recognises that on our own we can never live in conversion. This is not the fruit of good intentions, it is the first step of love: *A voice! My beloved!* (*Song* 2:8).

It can happen that, immersed in the flow of action, we stop calling out (*Lam* 5:21; cf. *Jer* 31:18) and listening to the voice that beckons: *Arise, my friend, my beauty, and come, soon!* (*Song* 2:10). Our frames of reference - thoughts, times of prayer, decisions, actions - no longer have a flavour of anticipation, of desire, of listening anew. We become preoccupied with other references and other necessities, which are not referred to Christ or to being conformed to him. The episode of the sons of Zebedee narrated in Matthew (*Mt* 20:17-28) is emblematic. It shows the two disciples covered with a shadow of subtle pettiness, even though they want to be close to Jesus. They followed, as we do, the Teacher, but their hearts were hardened. In a slow process, sometimes unnoticed, the heart becomes dry, it is unable to interpret according to wisdom, it becomes static and shrivelled, losing the contemplative gaze. It is not the hardness of heart of the atheist, it is the hardness of heart of the apostles, who were often, as Mark observed, reproved by Jesus: *Have you not yet understood, and do you not understand? Are your hearts hardened? Do you have eyes and see not, do you have ears and hear not?* (*Mk* 8:17-18).

We too, who follow Jesus according to the form of the Gospel, are subject to this gradual desiccation of heart. We are formally faithful, but worldly interests, reasoning, and valuations re-emerge in us. Contemplation is extinguished, beauty turns grey.

28. Pope Francis continually denounces the attitude of life that he calls worldliness: "[The Church] must strip away every kind of worldly spirit, which is a temptation for everyone; strip away every action that is not for God, that is not from God. . . strip away the seeming assurance structures

give, which, though certainly necessary and important, should never obscure the one true strength it carries within: God. He is our strength! To strip away what is not essential, because our reference is Christ."[61] In *Evangelii Gaudium* he warns: "Spiritual worldliness, which hides behind the appearance of piety and even love for the Church, consists in seeking not the Lord's glory but human glory and personal well-being. It is what the Lord reprimanded the Pharisees for: 'How can you believe, who receive glory from one another and do not seek the glory that comes from the only God?' (*Jn* 5:44). It is a subtle way of seeking one's 'own interests, not those of Jesus Christ' (*Phil* 2:21)".[62]

29. The spiritual journey sees no progress whatsoever if it does not open itself to the action of the Spirit of God through the effort of ascesis, and of spiritual combat in particular. "Our Lord adds that the way of perfection is narrow. With this expression he wants to teach us how the soul that wants to advance in this way must not only enter by the narrow gate, freeing itself from sensible goods, but also restrict itself, ridding itself and unburdening itself completely even of spiritual ones. . . . Since this is an effort in which God alone is sought and gained, it is God alone that one must seek and gain."[63] It is necessary to open the door and go out, seek in order to find, without fear of being struck: *I sought him, but I did not find him, I called him, but he did not answer me. . . they struck me, they wounded me, the guardsmen of the walls took my cloak away* (*Song* 5:6-7).

The constant call sounds out: "In fact the vocation of consecrated persons to seek first the Kingdom of God is first and foremost a call to complete conversion, in self-renunciation, in order to live fully for the Lord, so that God may be all in all. Called to contemplate and bear witness to the transfigured face of Christ, consecrated men and women are also called to a 'transfigured' existence."[64] The heart knows the wound and lives with it, while the Spirit deep within us opens us to contemplative prayer.

---

[61] Francis, address on the occasion of the meeting with the poor assisted by Caritas, Assisi, 4th October 2013.

[62] Francis, apostolic exhortation *Evangelii Gaudium* (24th November 2013), 93; cf. 93-97.

[63] St John of the Cross, *Ascent of Mount Carmel* 2, 7, 3.

[64] John Paul II, post-synodal apostolic exhortation *Vita Consecrata* (25th March 1996), 35.

CONTEMPLATE

THE BEAUTY THAT RENEWS

30. Prayer is situated between our weakness and the Spirit. Yearning, seeking, exercise, journey: it wells up from the depths of the person as from a wound inflicted by grace. Like a spring of living water it transports, drives, excavates, *wells up* (cf. *Jn* 4:10), brings to flower. Prayer is an inner birth: we become aware of a life present in us, that germinates and grows in silence. For mystics, praying means perceiving our deepest reality, the point at which we connect with God, where God touches us while he recreates us: the sacred place of encounter; the place of new life. *Behold, the winter is past. . . the flowers have appeared in the fields. . . The fig has put out its first fruits and the flowering vines emit fragrance* (*Song* 2:11a, 12a, 13a). One must approach this place with the will and fidelity of one who loves: *Tell me, O love of my soul, where you go to pasture the flock, where you make it lie down at midday, so that I may not be as a vagabond behind the flocks of your companions* (*Song* 1:7). In the much-admired Sistine Chapel fresco of the Creation, Michelangelo has us contemplate the finger of the Father that grazes the finger of Adam, thus hinting at a mystery. The communion once begun will have no end.

31. Prayerful contemplation is the seal of the Beloved: pure grace in us. The only attitude is a waiting that is like a cry. Biblical language and that of the fathers used the verb *hypoménein* and the substantive *hypomoné*: to stand beneath, to huddle up and be still, waiting for something to happen to us. The cry for help: *Out of the depths I call to you, O Lord!* (*Ps* 129:1) dares to express with a cry before the face of God my desperation, my desire to contemplate his face. The monks began to use the name of Jesus as a supplication: "Jesus, help me! Jesus, save me! Jesus, mercy!" The soul pitches its tent and dwells in the Name, dwells in love. It contemplates.

32. Prayer thus leads us back to the centre of our being; it entrusts us to Jesus while it heals our ego, and restores our unity: "The divine Teacher is in the depths of our soul as in the hull of Peter's boat. . . Sometimes it seems that he is sleeping, but he is always there; ready to save us, ready to hear our request."[65]

---

[65] Blessed Charles de Foucauld, *Opere spirituali*, (Rome, San Paolo Edizioni, 1997), p. 144.

St John of the Cross sings: "What more do you want, O soul, and why do you still seek outside of yourself, when you have inside yourself all your wealth, your delights, your satisfaction, your abundance and your kingdom, meaning the Beloved, whom you desire and crave? Rejoice and be glad with him in your interior recollection, because you have him so close! Here you desire him, you adore him, without going to seek him elsewhere, because you would become distracted, you would grow weary without being able to find or enjoy him with greater certainty and speed, nor have him closer than inside of you".[66] The Byzantine tradition uses a figurative expression: the mind (*noûs*) descends into the heart. The intellect abandons its own cogitations and unites itself with the heart that pleads: *Place me as a seal upon your heart, as a seal upon your arm, because love is as strong as death as tenacious as the kingdom of the dead is passion: its flames are flames of fire, a holy blaze!* (*Song* 8:6). The whole being enters into the life of God, is healed and integrated with the action of the Spirit: Love restores its beauty. Contemplation becomes a wound of the Beloved who recreates us, a presence that dwells within us:

> O flame of living love,
> that amorously wounds
> the deepest centre of my soul!
> Since you are no longer painful,
> if you wish, you may finish now,
> tear the veil of this sweet encounter.[67]

---

[66] St John of the Cross, *Spiritual Canticle* B, strophe I, 8.
[67] Ibid., *Living Flame of Love* B, Prologue, 4.

AN EXERCISE OF TRUTH

33. Beauty is the "splendour of truth", "effoliation and exercise of being", as affirmed by the ancient philosophy revived by Thomas, which is to say that it makes manifest the reality of life that each person bears within him: the Truth. The mystery of being presents itself to our awareness as beauty that generates wonder and amazement. We are struck not by the comprehensible, but by what is beyond our comprehension; not the quantitative aspect of nature but its quality; not that which extends beyond time and space, but rather the true significance, the source and end of being: in other words, the indescribable.[68] It is life that shines out, manifests itself, overflows, in spite of the veils behind which it is hidden and guarded. In order to intuit the ineffable and grasp its essence, it is necessary that our hearts live in the mystery, but at the same time live within history in a contemplative way.

We call our life "consecrated", and perhaps this adjective risks losing the living lustre of the mystery that dwells within it and, in an everyday manner, manifests itself in it. Our consecrated life, in fact, expresses a style, a way of living in the world: it has a task that is at the same time both heuristic (it finds, discovers, makes visible) and hermeneutic (it interprets, explains, makes understood).

HOLINESS THAT WELCOMES

34. The Christian tradition reckons up its uniqueness - in its way of life and its form - and, in understanding the faith that gives rise to it, finds itself able to assume conditions imposed by history and cultures. The unity between the mission of Christ and his life is made incarnate in the Christian style and form in every moment of history.

Let us examine the way of life of Christ. This expresses the unique capacity of Jesus to dwell within the Father in the love of the Spirit, while he learns from every individual and from every situation (cf. *Mk* 1:40 f.; 5:30; 7:27-29). This attitude is not a sign of weakness, but of authority, strength and holiness. He is luminous because he is at prayer; thoughts,

---

[68] Cf. Abraham Joshua Heschel, *L'uomo alla ricerca di Dio* (Comunità di Bose, Edizioni Qiqajon, 1995).

words, actions harmonise and manifest the simplicity and unity of his being. His splendour as Son of the Father does not dazzle, but approaches us in a discreet way, sets itself aside for the sake of all. He creates spaces of freedom around himself, communicating with his presence alone a benevolent nearness. In this encounter, people are placed in the condition to discover their deepest identity. They recognise their own truth: the mystery of being sons and daughters of God.

Christ's way of life emphasises the fact that he looks with the eyes of God who is love. Those who have encountered Jesus are able to resume the journey, because what is essential to their existence has been unveiled and is therefore known. The man Jesus of Nazareth told us about God, and it is in him that *the fulness of divinity dwells bodily* (*Col* 2:9). It is the man Jesus of Nazareth whom consecrated persons are called to follow in a personal and communal life, that is above all human and humanised.

Christ teaches us to live in this world with sobriety, with justice and piety (*Titus* 2:12). In this way, our humanity is purified and enlivened by the demands of contemplation, and is freed on a daily basis from deception, so as to become a human and holy place that welcomes. It becomes an echo and recounting of the life of Jesus, albeit within limitations and finitude. Let us learn the way of life that the *Didaché* calls "the ways of the Lord".[69] The *sequela Christi,* Pope Francis reminds us, find in the holy humanity of Christ the model for their own humanity so as to bear witness how he "lived upon this earth".[70]

THE LISTENING THAT SEES

35. Christ's way of life is learned by listening. We are called to the effort of a contemplative way of life in which the Word may shine out in our lives as men and women: in thought, in silent prayer, in fraternity, in our encounters and service, in the places in which we live and proclaim the grace of mercy; in choices, in decisions, in formative journeys pursued in a constant and fruitful way.

In listening to the Word of God, the consecrated person finds the place in which he puts himself under the gaze of the Lord and learns from him to

---

[69] *Didaché*, 11, 8.
[70] Antonio Spadaro, "Svegliate il mondo!". Conversation of Pope Francis with superiors general, in *La Civiltà Cattolica*, 165 (2014/I), 7.

look at himself, at others, and the at world. The *Letter to the Hebrews* (4:13) effectively demonstrates this crossing of glances: *Before the Word of God* (lógos toû theoû) *there is no creature that can hide itself, but everything is naked and uncovered to his eyes and we must give an account to him* (ho lógos). The Word sees us, looks at us, regards us, engages and involves us; and *his eyes are like a flame of fire* (cf. *Rev* 19:12).

Christian contemplation is born and grows in the exercise of a form of listening that is obedient (*obaudire*) and uninterrupted. If God is the one who speaks, the believer is someone called to listen, and the contemplative a person who listens incessantly. We see by hearing within a relationship of covenant, of completion, of joy. An active exercise, this love and desire for the true: *Listen to my voice! And I will be your God and you will be my people; walk always on the path that I will show you, so that you may be happy* (*Jer* 7:23).

36. This synthesis between hearing and seeing "becomes possible through the person of Christ himself, who can be seen and heard. . . St Thomas Aquinas speaks of the apostles' *oculata fides* - a seeing faith! - in the presence of the body of the Risen Lord. With their own eyes they saw the risen Jesus and they believed; in a word, they were able to peer into the depths of what they were seeing and confess their faith in the Son of God, seated at the right hand of the Father. . . Only when we are configured to Jesus do we receive the eyes needed to see him".[71] Called to listen, may we cultivate *a docile heart* (*1 Kings* 3:9), and let us ask for wisdom and understanding (cf. *1 Kings* 3:12) in order to discern what comes from God and what is contrary to it.

Listening to the Word presupposes vigilance (cf. *Rev* 2:1-3), attention to what is heard (cf. *Mk* 4:24), awareness of the one who is heard (cf. *Jer* 23:16) and of how one listens (cf. *Lk* 8:18). Teresa of Avila recalls: "We in fact do not call prayer, that of one who does not consider with whom he speaks, who is speaking, what he asks, and of whom he asks it".[72]

This exercise permits the illumination of the *chaos* of one's own ego, accepting the mysterious and compassionate, albeit demanding, gaze of Christ the Lord who leads the consecrated person to a realistic vision of

---

[71] Francis, encyclical letter *Lumen Fidei* (29th June 2013), 30-31.
[72] St Teresa of Avila, *Interior Castle*, *First Mansion*, I, 7.

self: "Set your eyes on him alone. . . if you set your eyes on him, you will find everything there".[73]

37. In his *Rule*, Benedict made the tax collector in the parable of Luke (cf. *Lk* 18:9-14) the model of the monk, his *exemplum*.[74] He does not ask for monks with their eyes set on the heavenly heights, but with their eyes bent toward the ground. The monk does not proclaim his own closeness to the Lord, but recognises his distance from him; he does not pronounce a magniloquent prayer, but confesses his own sin: *O God, have pity on me, a sinner*.[75] Isaac of Nineveh writes: "He who has been made worthy of seeing himself is greater than the one who has been made worthy of seeing the angels. . . He who is sensitive to his sins is greater than he who raises the dead with his prayer".[76] Pope Francis affirms with fine realism: "If one does not sin, one is not human. We all make mistakes and we must recognise our weakness. A consecrated person who recognises that he is weak and a sinner does not contradict the testimony that he is called to give, but rather reinforces it, and this is good for everyone".[77]

QUIES, REQUIES, OTIUM

38. In order to dwell in relationship with God, in the power of the Spirit, it is necessary to give oneself time and space, going against the tide. The culture of the present time does not believe in the processes of life and change, even if scientifically it places them at the foundation of its vision. What has value is whatever comes about rapidly, begins immediately, moves quickly. There is no appreciation for the epilogue: every dynamic thing flashes and is consumed in the present moment.

In the Christian way of living, time is not a commodity, but a sign that reveals God to us here and now. Adequate space and time are necessary, as places to be inhabited without breathless haste.

---

[73] St John of the Cross, *Ascent of Mount Carmel*, II, 22.

[74] Cf. St Benedict, *Rule*, VII, 62-66.

[75] The brief prayer in the mouth of the tax collector has been called "the perfect and perpetual prayer": André Louf, *À l'école de la contemplation* (Paris, Lethielleux, 2004), 22.

[76] Isaac of Nineveh, *Un'umile speranza*. Anthology edited by S. Chialà, (Comunità di Bose, Edizioni Qiqajon, 1999), 73.

[77] Antonio Spadaro, "Svegliate il mondo!". Conversation of Pope Francis with superiors general, in *La Civiltà Cattolica*, 165 (2014/I), 5.

To describe the contemplative life, Western monastic tradition has often used terms that indicate interior activity, the time dedicated only to God: *vacare Deo*; finding repose in God, *quies, requies*; abstaining from active work in order to be able to work in the soul, *otium negotiosum*. These terms speak of rest and of quiet. In reality, they presuppose the effort of work and of interior combat: "Idleness hurts everything. . . but none so much as the soul".[78]

The inner life demands an ascesis of time and of the body. It requires solitude as an essential element of personal purification and integration; it calls to hidden prayer, so as to encounter the Lord who dwells in secret and make one's own heart the private room (cf. *Mt* 6:6), a highly personal and inviolable place in which to worship (cf. *1 Pet* 3:15): *Come, my beloved, into your garden, and eat of its exquisite fruits* (*Song* 4:16).

39. We often prefer to live outside of ourselves, outside the interior castle, as men and women of the superficial, because the adventure of the depths and the truth is frightening. We prefer ideas that are reassuring, even if limited, to a challenge that launches us beyond what can be glimpsed: "Yes, we know that we have a soul, because we have sensed it and because the faith teaches us this, but we content ourselves with a vague overview, so much so that we very rarely think of the riches that are within her, of her great excellence and of him who dwells within her. And this explains our great negligence in attending to the preservation of her beauty".[79]

Sometimes, we cannot find the dogged determination needed for the voyage to the depths that, through the shadows of limitation and sin, lead us to the ultimate truth that dwells within us: "We can consider our soul as a castle made of a single diamond or a very clear crystal, in which there are many mansions, as there are many in heaven. . . what is the soul of the just man if not a paradise, where the Lord says he takes his delights? So what will the room be like that is able to bring delight to a King who is so powerful, so wise, so pure, so full of riches? No, there is nothing that can be compared with the great beauty of a soul and with its immense capacity!"[80]

---

[78] St John Chrysostom, *Homilies on the Acts of the Apostles*, 35, 3.

[79] St Teresa of Avila, *Interior Castle*, First Mansions, I, 3.

[80] Ibid., I, 2.

THE INEFFABLE MEMORY

40. The way of the Word is the first path on which the Lord himself comes to us "when we are gathered by his love" for the holy supper; "and when, as once for the disciples" on the road to Emmaus, "so now for us, he opens the Scriptures and breaks the bread."[81] Word, Gospel: an open chest, a sublime treasure, God's narrative.[82] An encounter with someone always takes place by means of a word, which in making us participants in his life reveals to us something about ourselves.

Behold Jesus, *Agnus Dei*. The invisible face of Christ, the Son of God, is unveiled in the simplest and at the same time indescribable way, as he manifests himself in the mystery of his Body and Blood. The Church, in responding to the desire of men in every age, who ask to *see Jesus* (*Jn* 12:21), repeats the action that the Lord himself performed: it breaks the bread, offers the chalice of wine. "Behold the Christ in a bit of bread: in a crumb of created matter behold the Uncreated; behold the Invisible in a moment of the visible".[83]

Here the eyes of those who seek him with a sincere heart are opened; in the Eucharist the gaze of the heart recognises Jesus.[84] St John Paul II reminds us: "To contemplate Christ involves being able to recognise him wherever he manifests himself, in his many forms of presence, but above all in the living sacrament of his body and his blood. The Church draws her life from Christ in the Eucharist; by him she is fed and by him she is enlightened. The Eucharist is both a mystery of faith and a 'mystery of light'. Whenever the Church celebrates the Eucharist, the faithful can in some way relive the experience of the two disciples on the road to Emmaus: '*their eyes were opened and they recognised him*' (*Lk* 24:31)."

The Eucharist introduces us on a daily basis to the mystery of "the spousal meaning of God's love. As the Redeemer of the world, Christ is the Bridegroom of the Church. The Eucharist is the Sacrament of our

---

[81] *Roman Missal*, Eucharistic Prayer for Various Needs.

[82] Cf. Francis, apostolic exhortation *Evangelii Gaudium* (24th November 2013), 174-175.

[83] P. Mazzolari, *Il segno dei chiodi*,(Bologna, Dehoniane, 2012), 73-78.

[84] Cf. John Paul II, homily for the Solemnity of Corpus Christi, Basilica of St John Lateran (14th June 2001).

Redemption. It is the Sacrament of the Bridegroom and of the Bride."[85] It tells our heart that God is love.

41. Living the contemplative capacity of consecrated life means living eucharistically, in the way of life shown by the Son given for us. The Eucharist nourishes the *Jesu dulcis memoria*, an invitation for us consecrated men and women so that in the Holy Spirit (cf. *Jn* 14:26) the *memoria* of Jesus may dwell within the soul, in its thoughts and desires, as contemplation that transfigures our life and strengthens joy. "From the time in which I knew you, you have dwelt within my memory and it is here that I find you when I remember and rejoice in you",[86] St Augustine affirms, while the Greek Fathers indicate the continual memory of Jesus as a spiritual fruit of the Eucharist. In this assiduous remembrance of Jesus, thoughts of gentleness and benevolence blossom, while God takes up his dwelling within the soul and makes it his own through the work of the Holy Spirit.

42. Invocation and prayer, listening to the word of God, spiritual combat, and the sacramental celebration renew every day our openness to the gift of the Spirit: "Prayer, fasting, vigils and the other Christian practices, as good as they may seem to be in themselves, do not constitute the end of Christian life, even if they assist in reaching it. The true end of Christian life is the acquisition of the Holy Spirit of God."[87]

Benedict XVI described the inseparable preciousness of communion and contemplation: "Communion and contemplation cannot be separated, they go hand in hand. If I am truly to communicate with another person I must know him, I must be able to be in silence close to him, to listen to him and look at him lovingly. True love and true friendship are always nourished by the reciprocity of looks, of intense, eloquent silences full of respect and veneration, so that the encounter may be lived profoundly and personally rather than superficially. And, unfortunately, if this dimension is lacking, sacramental communion itself may become a superficial

---

[85] John Paul II, apostolic letter *Mulieris Dignitatem* (15th August 1988), 26.

[86] St Augustine, *Confessions*, X, 8-24.

[87] I. Gorainoff, *Serafino di Sarov: vita, colloquio con Motovilov, scritti spirituali*, (Torino, Gribaudi, 2006), 156.

gesture on our part. Instead, in true communion, prepared for by the conversation of prayer and of life, we can address words of confidence to the Lord, such as those which rang out just now in the Responsorial Psalm: 'O Lord, I am your servant; I am your servant, the son of your handmaid. / You have loosed my bonds. / I will offer to you the sacrifice of thanksgiving / and call on the name of the Lord' (*Ps* 116[115]:16-17)."

FORMATION

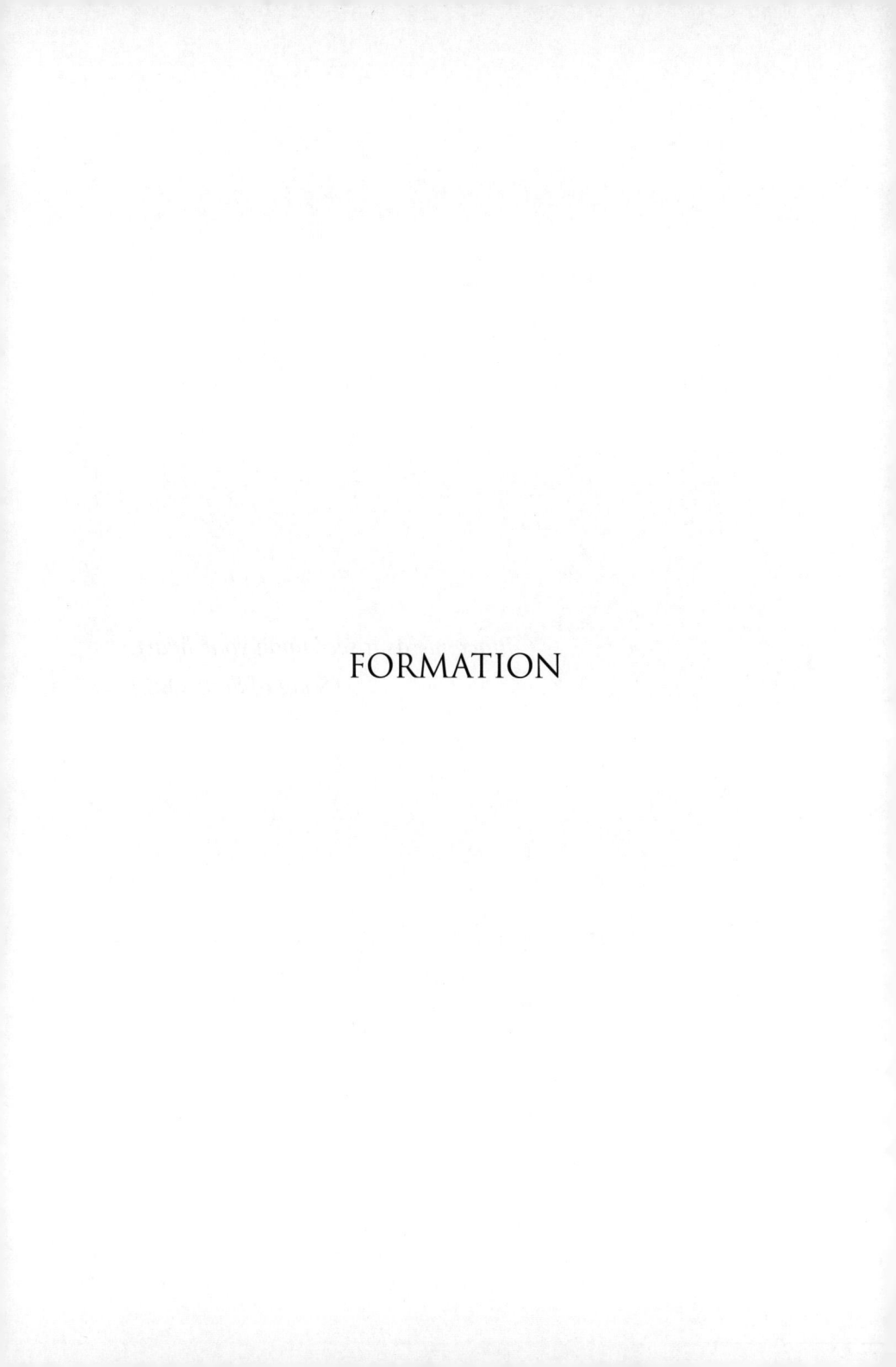

Place me as a seal upon your heart.
   (Song of Songs 8:6)

LISTENING

43. The words of the *Song of Songs* tell of a love directed toward an interpersonal relationship, decentralised, intent on contemplating the face of the beloved and hearing his voice (cf. *Song* 2:14): "He who loves must as a result cross the frontier that encloses him within his own limitations. This is why it is said of love that it melts the heart: that which is melted is no longer confined within its own limits."[88]

Overcoming one's own limits and boundaries ushers one into the dynamism of contemplation, where what speaks is only the beauty and power of love. Contemplation prevents union from being merely an indistinct and vague fusion, because it preserves otherness and makes giving possible. It is ecstasy before the "sacred ground of the other",[89] it is settling into the space of welcome and sharing what the other offers so as to recognise him in his uniqueness: *My dove, my all, is only one* (*Song* 6:9), or, again, *My beloved. . . is distinguished among a myriad* (*Song* 5:10). In order to remain in this epiphany, one must train one's eyes and heart to savour beauty as a mystery that envelops and engages.

44. One of the adjectives that permeates the *Song* is precisely the adjective *yāpâ*, "beautiful", and *yāfeh*, "handsome". In the Bible, the voice of a person is beautiful (*Ez* 33:32), a woman (Sarai the wife of Abram in *Gen* 12:11), the tree in Eden is beautiful to look at because it is desirable (*Gen* 3:6); the sandals of Judith captivate the eyes of Holofernes, but her beauty conquers his heart (*Judith* 16:9), the stones of the Temple are beautiful (*Lk* 21:5). Biblical beauty does not suggest only something physical, but also something interior: the wine that Jesus gives at Cana (*Jn* 2:10) is beautiful, in fact, as is the shepherd who gives his life for his sheep (*Jn* 10:11,14); the woman who anoints Jesus and receives his praise guaranteeing her eternal remembrance (*Mt* 26:10) performs a beautiful action.

Beauty in the Bible therefore appears as the "signature" of divine and human gratuitousness, and in the *Song* it presents itself as the overcoming of solitude, and as an experience of unity. The two who love each other

---

[88] St Thomas Aquinas, *Commentary on the Sentences of Peter Lombard* III XXV, I, I, 4 m.
[89] Francis, apostolic exhortation *Evangelii Gaudium* (24th November 2013), 169.

feel united even before they are, and after their union they want this to endure. They do not want to give each other only a fleeting emotion, but rather to savour the taste of eternity through a mark, a seal (*hôtâm*) on the heart and on the flesh (*Song* 8:6). This interprets everything in the *perspective of the forever* of God. This sign in the flesh is a wound that brings the eternal desire for love, a fire that great waters cannot extinguish (*Song* 8:7): "You, eternal Trinity, are a deep sea, so that the more I enter in the more I find, and the more I find the more I seek of you. You are insatiable, because although the soul may be satisfied in your abyss, nonetheless it is not entirely satisfied, but always remains hungry for you, eternal Trinity, desiring to see you with the light in your light."[90]

When we mature in our relationship with God, we permit him to purify us and teach us to see as he sees, to love as he loves. Of course, this way of seeing and loving is burdensome for a person - it means acquiring what Benedict XVI calls "a heart that sees"[91] - because it requires a radical transformation of the heart, what the fathers called *puritas cordis*, and this is a formative journey.

BEAUTY'S WAY OF LIVING

45. In the variety of cultural situations and models of life, consecrated life today requires attention and trust in personal and communal formation, and in particular in the dynamic of the institute, in order to introduce, accompany, sustain the contemplative attitude and capacity. There is a need to ask questions about our existence and to examine our *ethos* of formation. For instance, have we "the ability to establish a method characterised by spiritual and pedagogical wisdom, which will gradually lead those wishing to consecrate themselves to put on the mind of Christ the Lord. Formation is a dynamic process by means of which individuals are converted to the Word of God in the depths of their being."[92] We may need to rediscover in continual formation the breadth of the mystery

---

[90] St Catherine of Siena, *The Dialogue of Divine Providence* (Siena, Cantagalli, 2006), 402-403.

[91] Benedict XVI, encyclical letter *Deus Caritas Est* (25th December 2005), 31.

[92] John Paul II, post-synodal apostolic exhortation *Vita Consecrata* (25th March 1996), 68.

that dwells within us and transcends us: "Like a tree uprooted from the ground, like a river removed from its source, the human soul wilts away if it is cut off from that which is greatest in her. Without holiness, the good is shown to be chaotic; without the good, beauty becomes accidental. The Good and the Beautiful instead are radiant with a single voice."[93]

46. What way of life expresses in a simple and immediate way consecrated life in the everyday? Consecrated men and women: beyond doctrinal hermeneutics, magisterial supports, Rules and traditions, what story do they tell in the Church and in the human city? Are they truly a parable of evangelical wisdom and a prophetic and symbolic spur towards a "different" world? We call for a targeted and truthful evaluation of the way of life lived every day, so that the winnowing fan of wisdom may separate the chaff from the grain of wheat (cf. *Mt* 3:12), so the truth of our life and the call to Beauty that transfigures may be seen.

We will mention a few prompts for reflection, which, if integrated into our plans and formation practices, can accompany the vital process that from the surface leads to the depths of emotion, where the love of Christ touches the root of our being.[94]

MYSTICAL PEDAGOGY

47. We have described the Word of God (the first source of all Christian spirituality, nourishing a personal relationship with the living God and with his salvific and sanctifying will[95]) and the Eucharist (in which Christ himself is contained, our Passover and living Bread, the heart of ecclesial life and of consecrated life[96]) as places in which to dwell with humility of spirit so as to be formed and sanctified by them. We call for careful instruction to accompany the grace of these mysteries. The fathers especially loved mystagogical discourse, through which life was discovered and internalised, in the light of the Scriptures, and the sap of

---

[93] Abraham Joshua Heschel, *L'uomo alla ricerca di Dio* (Comunità di Bose, Edizioni Qiqajon, 1995), 141.
[94] Cf. John Paul II, post-synodal apostolic exhortation *Vita Consecrata* (25th March 1996), 18.
[95] Cf. ibid., 94.
[96] Cf. ibid., 95.

the truth pressed out from the celebrated mystery. Thus, as the Greek term *mystagogía* suggests, homiletic action and the liturgy could initiate, guide, and lead to the mystery. Mystagogical discourse can fruitfully introduce the men and women novices of our institutes and constantly accompany the formation of consecrated men and women, especially in liturgical life.

The liturgy itself is mystagogy - a discourse of words, actions, signs, and symbols of biblical origin - which introduces us into the life-giving fruitfulness of the *mystérion*. The category of *transfiguration* to which consecrated life is referred can stand at the heart of the mystagogical way. It must be able to evoke in the life of us believers the Paschal mystery, our destination at the resurrection.[97] The mystagogue *par excellence*, Gregory of Nazianzen declares, is Christ himself, and everything in the liturgy has as its subject him, the *Kýrios*, risen and present.

48. Mystagogical discourse is an eminently Christological action, because the intelligence of the Christian alone and the liturgical rites and actions alone are not enough to make the mystery understood and to participate in it fruitfully. There is no authentic Christian liturgy without mystagogy. If there is no mystagogical language in the liturgy, the same thing can take place that Origen says happens to the Levites charged with carrying the Ark of the Covenant enveloped in coverings and curtains. It can also happen to us, the consecrated, that we bear the mysteries of God upon our shoulders as a weight, without knowing what they are, and therefore without benefitting from them.[98]

We are called to perform a real evaluation of our community celebrations - the Liturgy of the Hours, daily and Sunday Eucharist, practices of devotion - asking ourselves if these are a lively and vitalizing encounter with Christ, "the source of her renewed self-giving".[99] This forms an invitation to think in a responsible way about a mystagogical pedagogy for our journeys of continual formation.

---

[97] Cf. Benedict XVI, apostolic exhortation *Sacramentum Caritatis* (22nd February 2007), 64: "'The best catechesis on the Eucharist is the Eucharist itself, celebrated well.' By its nature, the liturgy can be pedagogically effective in helping the faithful to enter more deeply into the mystery being celebrated".

[98] Cf. Origen, *Homilies on Numbers*, 5, 1.

[99] Francis, apostolic exhortation *Evangelii Gaudium* (24th November 2013), 24.

PASCHAL PEDAGOGY

49. The mystical journey at the foundation of our Christian life of special *sequela Christi* traverses the passion, death, and resurrection of the Lord. It requires special and continual care in each person's life so that we may welcome "the chance to be transformed by the Paschal experience, by being configured to the Crucified Christ who fulfils the Father's will in all things", and equal care in grasping the value and efficacy of fraternal and missionary life. The contemplative attitude nourishes itself on the veiled beauty of the cross. The Word that was with God, hung from the branches of the tree set up to connect heaven and earth, becomes the scandal *par excellence* before which we cover our faces. From the crosses of the world, today other victims of violence, almost other *christs*, hang humiliated, while the sun is obscured, the sea becomes bitter and the fruits of the earth that ripen for the hunger of all are shared out according to the greed of a few. An invitation is made to purify our gaze so we may contemplate the Paschal enigma of salvation living and active in the world and in our everyday surroundings.

Today, in the fraternities and communities that live immersed in contemporary cultures - cultures that have often become a marketplace of the ephemeral - sometimes even our gaze as consecrated men and women may lose the capacity to recognise the beauty of the Paschal mystery: the disarmed and defenceless composure that appears on the faces of brothers and sisters known to us, as it does also on those christs rejected by history whom we encounter in our charitable service. Faces *without appearance or beauty to attract our gaze, and find delight in them* (cf. *Is* 53:2).

50. Every day the spectacle of human suffering is bluntly exhibited. No redemption can be sought and understood, indeed, without confronting the scandal of suffering. This mystery traverses human history like an immense wave and calls us to reflect. Few have intuited better than Dostoyevsky the truest question that dominates the human heart: suffering, redemption from evil, victorious salvation over death. He set up a contrast between the significance of beauty and the mystery of suffering, asking for reasons. The young Ippolít, close to death, poses the decisive, terrible question to Prince Myshkin, protagonist of *The Idiot*, an enigmatic figure of Christ, the Innocent who suffers for the love of all: "Is it true, prince,

that once you said that the world will be saved by beauty? What is the beauty that will save the world?"[100]

The question about evil arises every day in the mind, in the heart, and on the lips of many of our brothers and sisters. Only if God makes his own the infinite suffering of the world abandoned to evil, only if he enters into the deepest darkness of human misery, is suffering redeemed and death defeated. This took place on the Cross of the Son. The suffering of Christ is able to explain the tragedy of humanity by extending it to the Godhead. In the suffering Christ we read the only answer possible to the question about suffering. The only way to contemplate, to understand the Beauty that dwells within us, is through the cross; one cannot attain to life except by going through death.

51. For us as consecrated persons, entering into Paschal wisdom and training to discover in all that which is disfigured and crucified, here and now, the transfigured face of the Risen One, is the serious business of faith. The contemplative journey is a Paschal journey. The Passover of Christ, the reason for our hope, scrutinises our fraternity and our mission, which are sometimes dimmed by superficial relationships, by routines without hope, by services that are solely functional, by eyes become lazy and no longer capable of recognising the mystery. In our communities, Beauty remains veiled! *We are foolish and slow of heart* (cf. *Lk* 24:25) in living the Paschal pedagogy. Sometimes we do not remember that participation in the Trinitarian communion can change human relationships, that the power of the reconciling action of grace breaks down the disintegrating dynamisms present in the heart of man and in social relationships, and that in this way we can point out to men both the beauty of fraternal communion and the ways that concretely lead to it.[101]

THE PEDAGOGY OF BEAUTY

52. Down through the centuries, consecrated life has been on an unending quest in the footprints of beauty, a watchful and fertile guardian of its sacredness. It has re-elaborated the vision, creating works that have

---

[100] Fyodor Dostoyevsky, *The Idiot*, II, 2.

[101] Cf. John Paul II, post-synodal apostolic exhortation *Vita Consecrata* (25th March 1996), 41.

expressed faith and the mysticism of light in architecture and in the creative arts and the arts of knowledge; in figurative, literary, and musical arts, always in search of new epiphanies of Beauty.[102]

Contemporary reflection, often in tension between the spiritualisation of nature and an aestheticisation of feeling, has ended up overlooking the cognitive and formative value of the beautiful, and the way it signifies truth, confining it to an ambiguous zone or relegating it to the ephemeral. We must restore the life-giving connexion with the ancient and ever-new significance of beauty as a visible and sensible site of the infinite mystery of the Invisible. Dwelling in this far-off place is like drawing from the wellspring of beauty. If existence does not participate in some way in this mystery, beauty remains unattainable: it is lost in a void of nonsense and in a void beyond all meaning.[103] More painful yet, we are deprived of it. Pope Francis, in his book *Beauty will save the world*[104] (written when he was Cardinal Archbishop of Buenos Aires) suggests a pedagogy of beauty, an educational experience in which the human person is seen as a bearer of the eternal, but one called to a process of life that flourishes in respect and in listening, and in integrating thought and emotion. These feelings ought to integrate themselves in maturity.

There needs, then, to be a twofold way of formation for the human *ethos*: "True knowledge means being struck by the arrow of beauty that wounds man, being touched by reality, by the *personal presence of Christ himself*, as he says. Being struck and conquered through the beauty of Christ is a knowledge more real and profound than mere rational deduction. We must foster the encounter of man with the beauty of faith. The encounter with Beauty can become the arrow that wounds the soul, and in this way opens its eyes, so much so that now the soul, on the basis of experience, has criteria of judgement and is also capable of correctly evaluating arguments."[105]

True and eternal beauty reaches the inner man by way of what can be called the spiritual "senses", of which Augustine speaks in analogy

---

[102] Cf. John Paul II, *Letter to Artists* (4th April 1999).

[103] Cf. N. Berdjaev, *The Meaning of the Creative Act*.

[104] Jorge Mario Bergoglio - Francis, *La bellezza educherà il mondo* (Bologna, EMI 2014).

[105] J. Ratzinger, *La corrispondenza del cuore nell'incontro con la Bellezza*, in 30 *Giorni*, no. 9, September 2002, 87.

with the senses of the body: "What is it I love when I love you? [. . .] In a certain sense I love light, sound, scent, food, embracing when I love my God; the light, sound, scent, food, embrace of my inner man, where upon my soul shines a light that has no limits of space, a sound that does not fade in time, a scent that the wind does not disperse, a taste that does not become nauseating with overeating, an embrace that satiety does not spoil. All this is what I love when I love my God."[106]

53. In our journey as Christians and consecrated people, we need to recognise the tracks left by Beauty, a path toward the Transcendent, towards the ultimate Mystery, towards God, precisely through its characteristic of opening and enlarging the horizons of human understanding, of taking it beyond itself, of putting it at the brink of the Infinite. We are called to travel the *via pulchritudinis*, which constitutes a journey that is at once artistic, aesthetic, and an itinerary of faith, of theological seeking.[107]

Benedict XVI heard in the grand musical tradition a reality on a theological level and made a response of faith, as he repeatedly said in commenting on concerts he attended: "He who has listened to this knows that the faith is true".[108] The beauty expressed in musical genius can be interpreted as a form of preparation for faith: "In that music, such an extraordinary power of Reality was perceptible as to make one realise, no longer through deduction but rather through an impulse of the heart, that this could not originate from nothing, but could be born only through the power of the Truth that is actualised in the inspiration of the composer."[109] Perhaps, as poetic and musical literature suggest, this is the reason why the great mystics loved to compose poems and canticles, to express something of the divine to which they had had access, in the soul's secret encounters.

Along with music come the arts of poetry and narrative, together with the figurative arts; all are possible ways of preparing for contemplation: from the pages of literature, to icons, to miniatures; from frescoes to paintings

---

[106] St Augustine, *Confessions*, X, 6, 8.

[107] Cf. Benedict XVI, address to artists in the Sistine Chapel (21st November 2009).

[108] J. Ratzinger, *La corrispondenza del cuore nell'incontro con la Bellezza*, in *30 Giorni*, no. 9, September 2002, 89.

[109] Ibid.

to sculptures. All "by an interior way, a way of self-transcendence and therefore, in this purification of the gaze, which is a purification of heart, reveal Beauty to us, or at least a ray of it. Precisely in this way it puts us in relationship with the power of the truth".[110]

In *Evangelii Gaudium*, Pope Francis emphasises the connection between truth, goodness, and beauty: there must be "a renewed esteem for beauty as a means of touching the human heart and enabling the truth and goodness of the Risen Christ to radiate within it."[111]

54. We are therefore called to make a harmonious journey, where the true, the good, and the beautiful can be blended in situations in which it would appear that duty, according to a misunderstanding of ethics, seems to have the upper hand.

The new digital culture and the new means of communication present a further challenge. These emphasise the language of the image, in constant flux with no possibility of meditation, without a destination and often without any hierarchy of values. There is an urgent challenge to cultivate a gaze that is present and reflexive, and can go beyond what is seen and the bulimia of immaterial contacts; a gaze that can usher us into the Mystery and bear witness to it. We are called to make journeys of formation to train ourselves to read inside of things, to travel the path of the soul that moves from the penultimate forms of beauty to the harmony of supreme Beauty. In this way we will realise "the hidden work of art that is the love story of each one of us with the living God and with our brothers, in the joy and hardship of following Jesus Christ in everyday life."[112]

THE PEDAGOGY OF THOUGHT

55. Forming a taste for the profound, for the interior journey, is thus indispensable. Formation is a demanding and fertile journey, never exhausted; its necessity is extinguished only by death.

Consecrated persons are called to exert themselves in "open thought": engaging with the cultures and values which we bear shapes our life to

---

[110] Ibid.
[111] Francis, apostolic exhortation *Evangelii Gaudium* (24th November 2013), 167.
[112] Benedict XVI, address to officials of the Pontifical Council for Culture, 15th June 2007.

accept differences and to see in them the signs of God. The intelligent and loving wisdom of contemplation trains us for a vision that is able to evaluate, accommodate, and situate every reality in Love.

In the encyclical *Caritas in Veritate*, Benedict XVI writes: "Paul VI had seen clearly that among the causes of underdevelopment there is a lack of wisdom and reflection, a lack of thinking capable of formulating a guiding synthesis, for which 'a clear vision of all economic, social, cultural and spiritual aspects' is required".[113] And he remarks: "Love in truth - *caritas in veritate* - is a great challenge for the Church in a world that is becoming progressively and pervasively globalised. The risk for our time is that the *de facto* interdependence of people and nations is not matched by ethical interaction of consciences and minds that would give rise to truly human development".[114] Pope Francis returns to this vital necessity in his conversation with superiors general of men's religious institutes, on 29th November 2013, referring to the challenge that complexity poses to consecrated life: "In order to understand we have to shake ourselves up, see reality from different points of view. We have to get used to thinking".[115]

We are called to constant attentiveness so as to create a fraternal and communal everyday setting, the first place of formation in which the growth of a pedagogy of thought may be fostered.

56. The service of authority makes a decisive contribution to this action. Continual formation requires in those who lead the institutes and communities a special focus, in the first place on the consecrated person, to direct him toward a sapiential attitude of life; to train him to the culture of the human as leading to Christian fulness; to permit him the exercise of reflection on values; to help him safeguard the sacredness of being, and not spend himself excessively in the name of efficiency and utility; to prevent Christian wisdom from being turned into a constellation of services and technical competencies. The one who serves in authority encourages and accompanies the consecrated person in the search for the

---

[113] Benedict XVI, encyclical letter *Caritas in Veritate* (29th June 2009), 31.
[114] Ibid.
[115] Antonio Spadaro, "Svegliate il mondo!". Conversation of Pope Francis with superiors general, in *La Civiltà Cattolica*, 165 (2014/I), 6.

metaphysical foundations of the human condition - the place where the Word makes his Light shine - so that "under the action of the Spirit, they resolutely keep times for prayer, silence and solitude, and they never cease to ask the Almighty for the gift of wisdom in the struggles of everyday life (cf. *Wis* 9:10)."[116]

In order to elicit and foster such a formational practice, it is not enough to make a few sporadic gestures or operational decisions. It is a matter of creating and sustaining a permanent practice that is able to influence the whole life of the community and the person. For this reason, it is necessary to focus on and adopt a way of life that may produce an environment whose habitual climate favours a sapiential, attentive and loving look at life and at people. We need a gaze aimed at discovering and living the opportunities of human and spiritual growth, a gaze that encourages the creation of new thinking, useful programmes, targeted pedagogy. We need to permit and facilitate the sort of introspection made up of self-reflection and existential engagement.

57. Eliciting a contemplative gaze likewise means encouraging the consecrated person to integrate his profound identity through appropriate reflection and reading, and by telling his own history as a "good" story, a positive thought, a relationship of salvation, and a human experience recapitulated in Christ Jesus: "The self is perceptible through interpretation of the traces that it leaves in the world."[117]

Our own story united with the stories of those who share our journey as brothers and sisters; the *semina Verbi* sown in the world today are a trace of God to be reread together, a grace of which to be aware. They are seed to be brought to germination as a new thought of the Spirit for us, so we may continue on the way. Pope Francis, addressing the community of writers of *La Civiltà Cattolica*, invited them to rediscover this pedagogy: "It is your duty to gather and express the expectations, aspirations, joys and dramas of our time and to indicate ways to read reality in the light of the Gospel. Today the important spiritual questions are more pressing than ever, but someone must interpret and understand them. With humble and open intelligence, 'seek and find God in all things', as St Ignatius wrote.

---

[116] John Paul II, post-synodal apostolic exhortation *Vita Consecrata* (25th March 1996), 71.
[117] P. Ricoeur, *Il tempo raccontato*, (Milan, Jaca Book, 1998), 376.

God is at work in the life of every person and in culture: the Spirit blows where he wills. Endeavour to find out what God has brought about and how to continue his action. Spiritual discernment... seeks to recognise in the human and cultural situation the presence of God's Spirit, the seed of his presence already sown in events, in sensibilities, in desires and in the heart's profound aspirations and in social, cultural and spiritual contexts."[118]

Cultivating thought, forming judgement, training in the wisdom of looking and refinement of emotions, in Christ's way of living (*Gal* 4:19), are ways of preparing for mission.[119]

MERCY IS CLOSE BY

58. One fruitful journey we may travel as an exercise in contemplation is one which calls us to closeness. This is a journey of encounter, in which faces seek and recognise each other. Every human face is unique and unrepeatable. The extraordinary diversity of our faces makes us easily recognisable in the complex social environment in which we live; it favours and facilitates recognition and the discovery of the other.

If the quality of collective co-existence "starts over again from the thou",[120] which means from giving value to the face of the other and to a relationship of closeness, Christianity reveals itself as the religion of the face, or of closeness and proximity. "In a culture paradoxically suffering from anonymity and at the same time obsessed with the details of other people's lives, shamelessly given over to morbid curiosity, the Church must look more closely and sympathetically at others whenever necessary."[121]

God heals the myopia of our eyes and does not allow our gaze to stop at the surface where mediocrity, superficiality and diversity find a home: God "cleans, gives grace, enriches and enlightens the soul, acting like the sun that with its rays dries, warms, beautifies, and illuminates."[122]

---

[118] Francis, address to the community of writers of *La Civiltà Cattolica*, 14th June 2013.

[119] Cf. John Paul II, post-synodal apostolic exhortation *Vita Consecrata* (25th March 1996), 103.

[120] Cf. E. Lévinas, *Etica e infinito. Il volto dell'altro come alterità etica e traccia dell'infinito* (Rome, Città Nuova, 1988).

[121] Francis, apostolic exhortation *Evangelii Gaudium* (24th November 2013).

[122] St John of the Cross, *Spiritual Canticle* B, 32, 1.

The contemplative person strives to look with the eyes of God upon humanity and upon created reality, to the point of *seeing the invisible* (cf. *Heb* 11:27), meaning the action and presence of God, always indescribable and visible only through faith. Pope Francis invites us to that spiritual intelligence and to that *sapientia cordis* which identify the true contemplative Christian as the one who knows how to be eyes for the blind, feet for the lame, speech for the dumb, father to the orphan and neighbour for the one who is alone, recognising in them the image of God.[123]

Christians "are first of all mystics with their eyes open. Their mysticism is not a natural mysticism without a face. It is, instead, a mysticism that seeks the Face, that leads to the encounter with those who suffer, to the encounter with the face of the unhappy and the victims. Open and vigilant eyes foment within us a rebellion against the absurdity of an innocent and unjust suffering; they awake in us a hunger and thirst for justice, for the great justice for all, and they prevent us from orienting ourselves exclusively within the minuscule criteria of our world of mere needs."[124]

59. Only love is capable of discovering that which is hidden: we are called to that wisdom of the heart which never separates the love of God from love for others, particularly for the poor, the least, "flesh of Christ",[125] the face of the crucified Lord. The consistent Christian lives each encounter with an attentive heart, so in addition to professional competence and training, formation of the heart is needed, so that faith may become active in love (cf. *Gal* 5:6): "The Christian's programme - the programme of the Good Samaritan, the programme of Jesus - is 'a heart which sees'. This heart sees where love is needed and acts accordingly. Obviously when charitable activity is carried out by the Church as a communitarian initiative, the spontaneity of individuals must be combined with planning, foresight and co-operation with other similar institutions."[126]

---

[123] Cf. Francis, message for the 23rd World Day of the Sick, 3rd December 2014.

[124] J.B. Metz, *Mistica dagli occhi aperti. Per una spiritualità concreta e responsabile*, (Brescia, Queriniana, 2011), 65.

[125] Cf. for example Francis, Vigil of Pentecost with the ecclesial movements, 18th May 2013; ibid., homily on the occasion of the canonisation of the martyrs of Otranto and of two Latin American blessed, 12th May 2013; ibid., *Angelus*, 11th January 2015.

[126] Benedict XVI, encyclical letter *Deus Caritas Est* (25th December 2005), 31.

This gaze influences our life together, above all where new vulnerabilities manifest themselves and ask to be accompanied with a "steady and reassuring pace".[127]

"For just as some people want a purely spiritual Christ, without flesh and without the cross, they also want their interpersonal relationships provided by sophisticated equipment, by screens and systems which can be turned on and off on command. Meanwhile, the Gospel tells us constantly to run the risk of a face-to-face encounter with others, with their physical presence which challenges us, with their pain and their pleas, with their joy which infects us in our close and continuous interaction. True faith in the incarnate Son of God is inseparable from self-giving, from membership in the community, from service, from reconciliation with others. The Son of God, by becoming flesh, summoned us to the revolution of tenderness."[128]

The face of the Father, in the Son, is the face of mercy: "Jesus of Nazareth, by his words, his actions, and his entire person reveals the mercy of God".[129] Every consecrated woman and man is called to contemplate and bear witness to the face of God as the One who *knows and understands our weaknesses* (cf. *Ps* 102), so as to pour the balm of closeness on human injuries, opposing the cynicism of indifference.

"Let us open our eyes and see the misery of the world, the wounds of our brothers and sisters who are denied their dignity, and let us recognise that we are compelled to heed their cry for help! May we reach out to them and support them so they can feel the warmth of our presence, our friendship, and our fraternity! May their cry become our own, and together may we break down the barriers of indifference that too often reign supreme and mask our hypocrisy and egoism!"[130] The contemplation of divine mercy transforms our human sensibility and enfolds it in the embrace of a seeing heart.

---

[127] Francis, apostolic exhortation *Evangelii Gaudium* (24th November 2013), 169.

[128] Francis, apostolic exhortation *Evangelii Gaudium* (24th November 2013), 88.

[129] Francis, *Misericordiae Vultus*, bull of indiction of the extraordinary jubilee of mercy (11th April 2015), 1.

[130] Ibid., 15.

FORMATION
IN THE DANCE OF CREATION

60. "Praise to you, my Lord, with all your creatures."[131] The canticle of Francis of Assisi continues to resound at the beginning of the twenty-first century with a voice that knows no weariness. It calls us to astonishment, and recognises the original beauty with which we are marked as creatures. In Francis of Assisi is fulfilled the perfect humanity of Christ in which *all things were created* (*Col* 1:16), the glory of God is resplendent, and the immense is glimpsed in the infinitely small.

The Lord plays in the garden of his creation. We can hear the echoes of that game when we are alone on a starry night, when we see children in a moment in which they are truly children; when we feel love in our hearts. In these moments the reawakening, the "newness", the void and the purity of the vision become evident. They allow us to glimpse a glimmer of the cosmic dance to the rhythm of silence, the music of the wedding feast.[132]

We are present in this dance of creation in the humble manner of cantors and custodians. Cantors: called to re-enliven our identity as creatures, we lift up our praise in the immense symphony of the universe. Custodians: we are called to watch over the beauty and harmony of creation, like watchmen awaiting the dawn. Pope Francis asks us to remember that we are not masters of the universe. He asks us to redesign our anthropological vision according to the vision of him who *moves the sun and the other stars*,[133] out of respect for our special dignity as human beings, creatures of this world who have the right to live and to be happy.[134]

Modern anthropocentrism has ended up placing technological prowess above reality in such a way as to diminish the intrinsic value of the world, in the complementarity of its order and of all creatures. On the human being, Pope Francis continues by citing Romano Guardini: "The technological mind sees nature as an insensate order, as a cold body of facts, as a mere 'given', as an object of utility, as raw material to be hammered into useful shape; it views the cosmos similarly as a mere

---

[131] St Francis of Assisi, *Canticle of the Creatures*, 1.

[132] Cf. Thomas Merton, *Seeds of Contemplation*.

[133] Dante Alighieri, *Divina Commedia*. Paradiso, XXXIII, 145.

[134] Cf. Francis, encyclical letter *Laudato Si'* (18th June 2015), 43.

'space' into which objects can be thrown with complete indifference."[135] We are living with an excess of anthropocentrism.

61. A new relationship with nature is not possible without a new heart, capable of recognising the beauty of every creature, the special dignity of human beings, the necessity of relationship, openness to a "thou" in which each recognises the same origin, the divine Thou. As consecrated persons we hear the call to reciprocity in relationships, to hearts capable of prayerful praise as the expression of an ascesis that calls to conversion, to a passage from the self-referentiality that makes us arrogant and closed off, liable to humiliate both people and nature, to the hospitable holiness of Christ in which all things are welcomed, healed and restored to their human and creaturely dignity.

Precisely by virtue of what heart's wise intelligence suggests to us, we hear the call to undertake choices, to take concrete actions as individuals, as communities, and as institutes so we may show forth a reasonable and just way of life.[136] We are invited with all our brothers and sisters in humanity to accept the "great cultural, spiritual and educational challenge [that] will demand that we set out on the long path of renewal".[137]

A NEW *PHILOKALIA*

62. There is still a pressing need for the continual formative act - a new *philokalia* - that can open us, support us, activate within us consecrated men and women the contemplative *habitus*: "By learning to see and appreciate beauty, we learn to reject self-interested pragmatism. If someone has not learned to stop and admire something beautiful, we should not be surprised if he or she treats everything as an object to be used and abused without scruple".[138] Pope Francis calls for passion in educational efforts according to an ecological spirituality that is "grounded in the convictions of our faith, since the teachings of the Gospel have direct consequences for our way of thinking, feeling and living."[139]

---

[135] Ibid., 115.
[136] Cf. ibid., 203-208.
[137] Ibid., 202.
[138] Ibid., 215.
[139] Ibid., 216.

This spirituality calls us to conversion and therefore to an ascesis in which, recognising our sometimes routine ways of life, we commit ourselves to exercises of deep transformation: "The external deserts in the world are growing, because the internal deserts have become so vast".[140] In order to make our desert fruitful, let us place within our interior, fraternal, and missionary life the seeds of caring, of tenderness, of gratitude, of gratuitousness, of the joy that is able to enjoy small and simple things, the savour of encounter, of service, "in developing their gifts, in music and art, in contact with nature, in prayer."[141]

In the time of creation, there was a seventh day on which God created rest. The enjoyment of rest seems not to affect us. We work with praiseworthy effort, but often this becomes the paradigm to which we attach our consecrated life. We are invited to rediscover the day of the Risen One in life and in our communities. It is the day of arrival and of new departure, but above all the day on which to remain in enjoyment of the splendour of the beloved Presence.

63. *Set me as a seal upon your heart* (*Song* 8:6), the bride in the *Song* asks, almost as if to imprison love in a bond of fidelity. The emphasis is on the care needed to accompany fidelity with the *sequela Christi* in our special consecration, in a time when this is often undermined by the fragility of our life in the Spirit (cf. *1 Thess* 5:17,19). The contemplative dimension of consecrated life will mature if formative spaces are opened. These are journeys that are chosen, wanted, and taken.

Let us therefore feel ourselves under examination concerning our *ratio formationis*, our formative practices and experiences, and concerning the context of formation in the various forms of consecrated life. Let us examine our everyday personal and fraternal life: our way of praying, of meditating, of studying, of living in relationship and in apostolic life; of resting. The contemplative attitude examines our surroundings and the dynamics of every day: our preferences, values, carelessness, methods, and customs, our various choices, decisions and cultures. Everything must be scrutinised in discernment and illuminated by the beauty of the

---

[140] Benedict XVI, homily on the occasion of the solemn beginning of the Petrine ministry, 24th April 2005.

[141] Francis, encyclical letter *Laudato Si'* (18th June 2015), 223.

Mystery that dwells within us. We must bear witness to this Light in humanity and among humanity: consecrated as a "'city on a hill', which testifies to the truth and the power of Jesus's words".[142]

---

[142] Francis, apostolic letter to all consecrated people on the occasion of the Year of Consecrated Life (21st November 2014), 2.

EPILOGUE

Come, my beloved!
(*Song of Songs* 7:12)

LISTENING

64. Love is an event that transfigures time by infusing an energy that is renewed even as it expends itself. It is characteristic of love to live in a dimension of expectation: to learn how to wait. This is the case of Jacob when he falls in love with Rachel: *Jacob loved Rachel. He therefore said [to Laban]: "I will serve you seven years for Rachel, your younger daughter"... So Jacob served seven years for Rachel: they seemed to him a few days, so great was his love for her* (Gen 29:18,20). Jacob makes his love for a beloved woman his reason to exist, and by virtue of this the fatigue of his work and time take second place. In the *Song*, the dimension of time seems to disappear. Love removes man from the tyranny of time and of things, and replaces the spatial-temporal co-ordinates - or, better, it gives them the oxygen of freedom, which gives primacy not to doing, but to dwelling, to contemplating, to welcoming.

One who loves is in haste to see the beloved face again; he knows that the joy of an encounter will follow endless desire. With the invitation to the beloved to flee *upon the mountain of spices* (*Song* 8:14), the poem reawakens the dynamic of desire and search, and celebrates in song the beloved beauty that can never be possessed except its otherness is recognised, an otherness of which the body is a symbol. The search begins again so that the two lovers may continue to call to one another without ceasing, setting free the cry that represents their most incisive appeal: *Come!* It is a voice that calls in the reciprocity of desire (*Song* 2:10,13; 4:8; 7:12), a call aimed at transcending one's own solitude: an invitation to communion.

In the spousal dynamic of consecrated life, this movement of the soul turns into incessant prayer. The Beloved is invoked as a presence operating in the world, a fragrance of the resurrection that consoles, heals, and opens to hope (*Jer* 29:11). Let us make our own the invocation that closes biblical revelation: *The Spirit and the bride say: "Come!" And he who hears repeats: "Come!"* (*Rev* 22:17).

CONTEMPLATE

ON THE MOUNTAIN, IN THE SIGN OF FULFILMENT

65. *"Come, let us go up to the mountain of the Lord and to the house of the God of Jacob, and he will teach us his ways* (*Is* 2:3). Attention, intention, will, thought, affections, emotions, all that is within me, come: let us go up to the mountain, to the place where the Lord sees and is seen".[143]

If the call to contemplation, the call to go up to the mountain of the Lord, is the same vocation as that of the Church, and every other activity is ordered and subordinated to it,[144] this acquires a permanent meaning and resonance for monastic communities, for praying communities completely dedicated to contemplation, according to the charism proper to each religious family.

Monastic life is the first form taken by communities of consecrated life in the Church, and still today it signifies the presence of men and women in love with God, who live in the search for his face and find and contemplate God in the heart of the world. The presence of communities set as cities on the hill and lamps on the lampstand (cf. *Mt* 5:14-15), albeit in simplicity of life, visibly depicts the destination to which the entire ecclesial community is walking, as she "advances down the paths of time with her eyes fixed on the future restoration of all things in Christ."[145]

What can they represent, for the Church and the world, these women and men who choose to live their lives on the mountain of intercession? What significance can a community have that essentially dedicates itself to prayer, to contemplation, in a context of evangelical *koinonia* and industriousness?

66. The life of contemplative persons stands as a symbol of love; these are men and women who live *hidden with Christ in God* (cf. *Col* 3:3), who inhabit the furrows of human history and, situated in the very heart of the Church and of the world,[146] remain "before God for all".[147]

---

[143] William of St Thierry, *The Contemplation of God*, Prologue, 1.

[144] Cf. Second Vatican Council, constitution on the sacred liturgy *Sacrosanctum Concilium*, 2.

[145] John Paul II, post-synodal apostolic exhortation *Vita Consecrata* (25th March 1996), 59.

[146] Second Vatican Council, dogmatic constitution on the Church Lumen Gentium, 44; John Paul II, post-synodal apostolic exhortation Vita Consecrata (25th March 1996), 3.29.

[147] E. Stein, Lettera a Fritz Kaufmann, in M. Paolinelli, *Stare davanti a Dio per tutti* (Rome, Il Carmelo di Edith Stein, OCD, 2013).

Prayerful communities do not set themselves up as a more perfect realisation of the Gospel, but constitute an instance of discernment at the service of the whole Church: a sign that indicates a journey, reminding the whole people of God of the meaning of that which it lives.[148] Consecrated in the fertile intimacy of intercession, communities of contemplative men and women are an image of the yearning for heaven, of God's tomorrow, the ardent expectation of the bride of the *Song*, "a sign of the exclusive union of the Church as Bride with her Lord, whom she loves above all things."[149] Contemplative communities are called to live the categories of a present already given[150] as mission, aware that present and eternity are no longer one after the other, but intimately connected.

The monastic vocation, Pope Francis has said, is "a tension between being hidden and being visible. The monastic vocation is this tension, tension in the fundamental sense, the tension of fidelity... Because your vocation is not a refuge; it is precisely going onto the battlefield, it is fighting, it is knocking at the heart of the Lord".[151]

Monastic *stabilitas* makes room for God and proclaims the certainty of his presence in the vicissitudes of human life, wherever this is found: wherever man dwells, there God has come to dwell, in his Son Jesus Christ. The perseverance of communities of contemplative men and women speaks of a place inhabited by those who do not pass by on the road, like the Levite or priest of the parable; a place inhabited by those who can live in a stable way so as to allow themselves to be encountered by man and by his questions, and thus accommodate wounded humanity in its relationship with God.

Speaking love to God and recounting to men a parable of the Kingdom of Heaven: this is the wholly contemplative life. Monks and nuns, as the context of their prayer, have the whole world: its noise and the silence of its desolation; its joys, riches, hopes, and anguish; its deserts of solitude and its anonymous crowds.

This is a journey made by pilgrims in search of the true God; it is the story of every contemplative person who remains watchful, while

---

[148] Cf. Second Vatican Council, decree on the renewal of religious life *Perfectae Caritatis*, 5.
[149] John Paul II, post-synodal apostolic exhortation *Vita Consecrata* (25th March 1996), 59.
[150] Benedict XVI, encyclical letter *Spe Salvi* (30th November 2007), 9.
[151] Francis, address to consecrated men and women of the diocese of Rome, 16th May 2015.

welcoming within himself the *sequela Christi* as configuration to Christ. *Stabilitas* nevertheless always reveals itself as a journey, a possibility of going beyond the boundaries of time and space, to become an outpost of humanity: "Let us go to die for our people", Edith Stein said to her sister Rose when she was arrested at the monastery in Echt and taken to Auschwitz.[152]

67. Monastic life, to a great extent adopting a feminine character, is rooted in a silence that becomes generative. "Understanding ourselves today as women of prayer is a great challenge", the nuns affirm, it is living a life-giving *stasis* that creates.

Women's monastic life becomes a heart of intercession, a story of true relationships, of care and healing: it is a custodian of every trace of life, capable of intuiting through empathy hidden and tenacious harmonies. Nuns know how to be, and are able to be, the voice of the gift freely given and of fertile questions, outside of all predetermined idealisations, while they allow themselves to be shaped by the power of the Gospel. The unification of the heart, a dynamic characteristic of monastic life, urgently requires that this life be set out anew as empathy, as a testing-place of histories of salvation, as somewhere consciously available for dialogue within the culture of fragmentation, of complexity, of precariousness, but yet somewhere fleeing from the fascination of an imaginary peace.

All of this requires a demanding formation in the life of faith, a life grown to maturity in docility to the Spirit. It likewise requires careful attention to the signs of the times, in a real relationship with history and with the Church in its particular realities, realities which are not composed simply of abstract information and relationships. It requires intercession able to rouse passion and permeate life; a landscape in which prophecy germinates.

68. From this frontier of human existence, contemplative communities become able to see beyond, of seeing the Beyond. Eschatology is the homeland not of those who leapfrog humanity, but of those who, in committing their whole lives to the absolute search for God, consult

---

[152] Last words of Edith Stein (St Teresa Benedicta of the Cross) to her sister Rosa at the monastery of Echt.

historical events in order to discern the traces of God's presence and serve his plans. Walls marking out space are at the service of seeking, of listening, of praise; they do not represent phobic separation or a dwindling of attention or acceptance: they express the essential pulse of strong love for the Church and supportive charity for our brothers.

Wholly contemplative life tells the story of the harmony between time and eschatology. Time becomes abridged. Discipleship and expectation walk together. The *follow me* of Jesus to the disciples is not sustainable without the parousia that becomes a cry in the Church's choral prayer, a hope that invokes: *Come, Lord Jesus* (*Rev* 22:20). The Bride Church is made fertile by the testimony of what lies beyond, because the eschatological dimension corresponds to the demand of Christian hope.

A contemplative community placed on a solitary mountain or among chaotic and noisy urban agglomerations remembers the vital relationship between time and the eternal. The community that contemplates recalls that we do not have infinite time at our disposal, an eternal return, a homogeneous continuum devoid of upheavals; it bears witness to a new revelatory possibility of time. Days are not an empty, dispersed, liquid eternity in which anything can happen except for one essential fact: that the eternal enter into time and give time to time. Time is lived as something substantial, full, replete with the eternal. Christian eschatology is no longer lived as an inert fragment in our brief times, but as continual and luminous evolution.[153] Contemplatives do not experience time as a reality made annoying by waiting, but as the continual flow of the Eternal in everyday time. It is a prophecy of life that continually commemorates the essential nexus that drives discipleship and expectation. Neither part can be eliminated without seriously compromising the other: one cannot live without breathing the infinite, without expectation, without eschatology.

69. This evangelical culture, so dear to the monasteries, has demonstrated over the centuries that Christian hope lived in proximate anticipation presents itself as an *opus Dei* that does not lead to historical and social disengagement, but generates responsibilities and sets the scene for a healthy humanism. In a culture that has generated the gloomy eschatology

---

[153] Cf. J.B. Metz, Tempo di religiosi? *Mistica e politica della sequela* (Brescia, Queriniana, 1978).

of boredom, time without time, that evades confrontation with transcendence, contemplative time can and must be vibrant; a time for those who have something else to say. By means of a life that is sober and joyous, prophetic, and by removing themselves from all manipulation and compromise, they attest to the precariousness and ephemeral character of every culture of the present that limits life.

Contemplative communities, in which men and women live the search for the face and listen to the *quotidie* Word, aware that God remains an infinity that is never knowable, are immersed in a dialectic of *already and not yet*. This logic touches not only the relationship between time and eternity, but also the relationship between the experience of the living God and the understanding of his mysterious transcendence. All of this played out in their own flesh, in the scarcity of things, in the flow of days and events.

Vigilant humanity, watchmen on the mountain who look for the glimmers of dawn (cf. *Is* 21:12), signal the *adventus* of the God who saves.

ON THE WAY TO GOD'S SAFEKEEPING

70. "The search for the face of God in everything, in everyone, everywhere, at any moment, discovering his hand in everything that happens: this is contemplation in the heart of the world",[154] wrote Blessed Teresa of Calcutta.

If communities entirely dedicated to contemplation light the way and guide our journey, the whole life of special consecration is a call to be a place where the embrace occurs and the companionship of God is given.

Authentically Christian contemplation cannot dispense with the movement toward the external, with a gaze that turns from the mystery of God to the world, and is translated into active compassion. No one has ever seen God (*Jn* 1:18), but Jesus has become his exegete, the visible face of the invisible Father. Only by engaging with Christ and his choices is it possible to contemplate. He who wants to contemplate God accepts living in such a way that permits the men and women of his time to recognise

---

[154] J.L. González Balado (ed.), *I fioretti di Madre Teresa di Calcutta. Vedere, amare, servire Cristo nei poveri*, (San Paolo, Cinisello Balsamo (MI) 1992), 62.

him. To those who live in bearing witness in the world, the God of Jesus Christ shows himself to be welcoming and companionable.

We are called to taste the mystery of the God who is *merciful and compassionate, slow to anger and rich in love and faithfulness* (*Ex* 34:6), of the God who *is love* (*1 Jn* 4:16), and to preserve his presence on the paths of humanity, including by the sign of fraternity.

Pope Francis invited consecrated persons in Korea: "You are challenged to become 'experts' in divine mercy precisely through your life in community. From experience I know that community life is not always easy, but it is a providential training ground for the heart. It is unrealistic not to expect conflicts; misunderstandings will arise and they must be faced. Despite such difficulties, it is in community life that we are called to grow in mercy, forbearance and perfect charity"[155] In this vision our fraternal life is sifted: a place of mercy and reconciliation, or an ineffective space and relationship permeated with distrust, judgement, even condemnation.

71. The event of contemplation can take place anywhere and at any time, on the solitary mountain or on the pathways of the edge of the non-human. And it brings salvation. The communities of consecrated men and women, standing on watch in the cities and at the frontiers among the peoples are places which sisters and brothers guarantee, for themselves and for the sake of all, a space for God's care. This extends an invitation to be praying communities in which God makes himself present; and is a reminder to live in watchful management of time so that it may not be filled with things, activities, words. Apostolic communities, fraternities, consecrated individuals in the various forms safeguard the time of God in the world, both in contact with cultures and in lasting encounters with them, the reasons and way of the Gospel: "Such communities are places of hope and of the discovery of the Beatitudes, where love, drawing strength from prayer, the wellspring of communion, is called to become a pattern of life and source of joy".[156] They are a sign of him who incessantly comes to encounter us as the Living One.

---

[155] Francis, address on the occasion of the meeting with religious communities in Seoul, Korea (16th August 2014).

[156] John Paul II, post-synodal apostolic exhortation *Vita Consecrata* (25th March 1996), 51.

At a time of bitter worldwide conflict (1943) and in a place, Auschwitz, in which everything proclaimed, or rather shouted, the death of God and of man, Etty Hillesum, a young Jewish woman, intuited with contemplative sight the intimate connection between the fate of the one and of the other, and rediscovered within herself the truth that the human being is the site of compassionate relationships in which God is still present. She set herself a task: to safeguard, to preserve, not just her physical life, but also her deepest core. This is the mystical experience that prayerful persons experience: "My God, these are times of such anguish. Tonight for the first time I lay awake in the darkness with my eyes burning, and before me passed image after image of human suffering. . . And with almost every beat of my heart, my certainty grew: . . . it is up to us to help you, to defend to the last your home within us. There exist persons who at the last moment worry about saving vacuum cleaners, silver forks and spoons, instead of saving you, my God. . . You have made me so rich, my God, allow me also to dispense to others by whole handfuls. My life has become an uninterrupted dialogue with you, a single great dialogue".[157]

When the spirit comprehends, sees and tastes the richness that is God himself, it spreads it as salvation and joy in the world. The promise of Isaiah comes true: *He will guide you always, the Lord will satisfy you in arid lands, he will refresh your bones; you will be like a watered garden and like a wellspring whose waters do not dry up* (*Is* 58:11-12).

72. Faithful contemplation, consistent in fulfilling its mission, has called consecrated men and women to the ultimate going out from self: "They lived and continue to live their consecration in prolonged and heroic suffering, and often with the shedding of their blood, being perfectly configured to the Crucified Lord".[158] This is the going out from self foreseen by Fr Christian de Chergé, prior of the Monastery of Tibhirine, decapitated together with six of his confrères in the Atlas mountains in Algeria, in May of 1996. These seven monks chose to bear witness to the God of life in silence and solitude, in everyday life with the people.

"My death may seem to prove right those who quickly saw me as a simpleton or an idealist: 'Now what do you have to say about it?' But they

---

[157] E. Hillesum, *Diario 1941-1943*, Adelphi, Milano 1996, 20th edition, 169-170; 682.
[158] John Paul II, post-synodal apostolic exhortation *Vita Consecrata* (25th March 1996), 86.

should know that at last my keenest curiosity will be satisfied. Behold, I will be able, if it pleases God, to immerse my gaze in that of the Father, to contemplate together with him his children as he sees them, completely illuminated by the glory of Christ, the fruit of his passion, transfixed by the gift of the Spirit, whose secret joy will always be that of establishing communion and re-establishing the likeness, playing with differences. For this lost life, totally mine, and totally theirs, I give thanks to God, who seems to have wanted it all and entirely for that *joy*, through and in spite of everything".[159]

Life becomes a song of praise, while contemplative prayer flows as a blessing, heals and restores, and opens to unity - beyond ethnicities, religions, cultures - while it ushers in the future fulfilment.

"My body is for the earth,
but please, no barrier between her and me.

My heart is for life,
but please, no affectation between her and me.

My arms for work,
they will be crossed very simply.

As for my face:
let it remain bare so as not to prevent the kiss
and the gaze, let it be seen".[160]

The eschaton is already present in history, a seed to be brought to fulfilment in the song of life that contemplates and accomplishes hope.

---

[159] C. de Chergé, *Testamento spirituale*, in *C. de Chergé e gli altri monaci di Tibhirine, Più forti dell'odio*, (Comunità di Bose, Edizioni Qiqajon, 2006), 219-220.
[160] Ibid.

FOR REFLECTION

NONFICTION

For Reflection

73. Thought-provoking ideas from Pope Francis:

– We too can consider: how does Jesus gaze at me today? How does Jesus look at me? With a call? With forgiveness? With a mission? . . . On the path that he made, we all are under Jesus's gaze: he always looks at us with love, asks us for something, forgives us for something and gives us a mission.[161]

– There are many problems that you encounter every day. These problems compel you to immerse yourselves with fervour and generosity in apostolic work. And yet, we know that by ourselves we can do nothing. . . The contemplative dimension of our lives becomes indispensable even in the midst of the most urgent and difficult tasks we encounter. The more our mission calls us to go out into the peripheries of life, the more our hearts feel the intimate need to be united to the heart of Christ, which is full of mercy and love.[162]

– May you continue on the journey of renewal that you have begun and, to a great extent, accomplished in these fifty years, examining every novelty in the light of the Word of God and listening to the needs of the Church and of the contemporary world, and using all the means and wisdom that the Church has made available to advance on the journey of your personal and community holiness. And among these means, the most important is prayer, even spontaneous prayer, prayer of praise and adoration. We consecrated men and women are consecrated to serve the Lord and to serve others with the Word of the Lord, are we not? Say to new members, please, say that praying is not a waste of time, adoring God is not a waste of time.

– Life is a journey toward the fulness of Jesus Christ, when the second coming occurs. It is a journey toward Jesus, who will come again in glory, as the angels said to the apostles on the day of the Ascension. Am I attached to my things, to my ideas, closed? Or am I open to the God of surprises? Am I a stationary person or a person on a journey? Do I believe in Jesus Christ and in what he has done? That he died,

---

[161] Francis, morning meditation in the chapel of the Domus Sanctae Marthae, 22nd May 2015.

[162] Francis, address on the occasion of the celebration of Vespers with priests, religious, seminarians, and lay movements, Tirana, 21st September 2014.

rose again... do I believe that the journey goes forth toward maturity, toward the manifestation of the glory of the Lord? Am I capable of understanding the signs of the times and of being faithful to the voice of the Lord that is manifest in them?[163]

– Often we make mistakes, for we are all sinners; however, we recognise we were wrong, we ask forgiveness and give forgiveness. And this does good for the Church: it makes the lymph of fraternity circulate in the body of the Church. And it also does good for the whole of society. This fraternity presupposes the paternity of God, and the maternity of the Church and of the Mother, the Virgin Mary. We must re-establish ourselves in this relationship every day, and we can do so with prayer, with the Eucharist, with adoration, with the Rosary. We thus renew our "being" with Christ and in Christ every day, and in this way place ourselves in an authentic relationship with our Heavenly Father and with Mother Church, our hierarchical Holy Mother Church, and Mother Mary. If our life always renews these fundamental relationships, then we are also able to achieve authentic fraternity, a testimonial brotherhood, which attracts.[164]

– God works, continues to work, and we can ask ourselves how we should respond to this creation of God, which is born of love, because he works through love. In the "first creation" we must respond with the responsibility that the Lord gives us: "The earth is yours, take it forward; let it grow". Even for us there is a responsibility to nurture the earth, to nurture creation, to keep it and make it grow according to its laws. We are the lords of creation, not its masters.[165]

– Every day you live the life of a person in the world, and, at the same time, retain contemplation. This contemplative dimension with the Lord and in relation to the world, to contemplate reality, to contemplate the beauty of the word as well as the great sins of society,

---

[163] Francis, morning meditation in the chapel of the Domus Sanctae Marthae, 13th October 2014.

[164] Francis, address to participants in the national assembly of the Italian Conference of Major Superiors (CISM), Vatican City, 7th November 2014.

[165] Francis, morning meditation in the chapel of the Domus Sanctae Marthae, 9th February 2015.

FOR REFLECTION

its deviations, all these things, and always in spiritual tension.... This is why your vocation is so fascinating, because it is a vocation which is spot on, where the salvation not only of people but of the institutions are at stake.[166]

– And to the work that the Holy Spirit does within us, of reminding us of Jesus's words, of explaining to us, of making us understand what Jesus said: how do we respond? . . . God is person: he is the person of Father, the person of Son, the person of the Holy Spirit. . . Our response to all three is to safeguard creation and make it flourish, to let ourselves reconcile with Jesus, with God in Jesus, in Christ, each day, and do not grieve the Holy Spirit, do not push him away: he is the guest in our heart, the One who accompanies us, who makes us grow.[167]

HAIL, WOMAN CLOTHED WITH THE SUN

74. Our thought turns to Mary, the ark of God. Next to her Child, flesh of her flesh and origin that comes from on High, Mary is united with the Mystery. Unspeakable happiness and an unfathomable enigma, she becomes a temple of silence without which the seed of the Word will not germinate, nor the astonishment over God and his wonders blossom. She is a place where are heard the vibrations of the Word, and the voice of the Spirit as a gentle breeze. Mary becomes the bride in an enchantment that loves. The divine event accomplished in her in an admirable way is welcomed into the bridal chamber of her life as a woman:

Adorna thalamum tuum, Sion,
Virgo post partum, quem genuit adoravit.[168]

Mary becomes a treasure-chest of memories concerning the Child, his deeds and words compared with the predictions of the prophets (cf. *Lk* 2:19), and ruminated over with Scripture in the depths of the

---

[166] Francis, audience with participants at the meeting organised by the Italian Conference of Secular Institutes, Vatican City, 10th May 2014.

[167] Francis, morning meditation in the chapel of the Domus Sanctae Marthae, 9th February 2015.

[168] *Liturgia Horarum*. Feast of the Presentation of Jesus in the Temple, Office of Readings, 1st responsorial.

heart. She jealously guards all she is not able to understand, waiting for the Mystery to be revealed. The Lucan account of the infancy of Jesus is a *liber cordis*, written in Mary's heart before it is on parchment. In these depths, every word of Mary, of joy, hope, suffering, has become a commemoration of God for assiduous contemplative rumination.

Over the course of the centuries, the Church has gradually come to understand the exemplary value of Mary's contemplation. Reading the Mother as an icon of contemplation has been the work of centuries. Denis the Carthusian indicates her as *summa contemplatrix* because just as "it was granted in a singular way that from her and by means of her the mysteries of human salvation should be realised, so also it was given to her in the most eminent and profound way to contemplate them."[169] From the annunciation to the resurrection, through the *stabat iuxta crucem*, where the *mater dolorosa et lacrimosa* acquires the wisdom of suffering and of tears, Mary wove the contemplation of the mystery that dwells within her.

In Mary we glimpse the mystical way of the consecrated person, established in the human wisdom that tastes the mystery of ultimate fulfilment. A woman clothed with the sun appears as a splendid sign in the heavens: *A great sign appeared in heaven: a woman robed with the sun, with the moon beneath her feet and on her head a crown of twelve stars (Rev* 12:1). She, the new Eve wedded beneath the cross, the new woman of the *Song,* comes from the desert leaning on her beloved (*Song* 8:5) and in the world and in the time of fragmentation and weakness she gives birth to the Son, the fruit of universal salvation, gladness of the Gospel that saves:

---

[169] S. de Fiores, *Elogio della contemplazione*, in S.M. Pasini (ed.), *Maria modello di contemplazione del mistero di Cristo*, (Rome, Ed. Monfortane, 2000), 21-22.

For Reflection

Go forth, we beseech you. . .
You will fly from spire to spire
around the cupolas,
you will enter by the arches of the churches
and behind the forests of skyscrapers,
into the heart of the palace
and in the midst of the steppe:
you will emigrate as a pilgrim and immediately
and everywhere you will give birth to your Son
joy and unity of things,
O eternal Mother.[170]

Vatican City, 15th October 2015
Memorial of St Teresa of Avila,
virgin and doctor of the Church

João Braz Card. de Aviz
Prefect

✠ José Rodríguez Carballo, O.F.M.
Secretary Archbishop

---

[170] D. M. Turoldo, *O sensi miei... Poesie 1948-1988* (Milan, Rizzoli, 1990), 256.